Firms, Industries, Markets

Clelia Mazzoni

Firms, Industries, Markets

Micro, Meso, and Macro Relationships in the *Economics of Complexity*

palgrave
macmillan

Clelia Mazzoni
University of Campania "Luigi Vanvitelli"
Capua, Italy

ISBN 978-3-031-59822-7 ISBN 978-3-031-59823-4 (eBook)
https://doi.org/10.1007/978-3-031-59823-4

This Palgrave Macmillan imprint is published by the registered company Springer Nature Switzerland AG.
The registered company address is: Gewerbestrasse 11, 6330 Cham, Switzerland

Paper in this product is recyclable.

To my son Ludovico
To my grandchildren Ambrogio and Elena

Foreword

Clelia Mazzoni's book stems from the idea that the relationship with the Task Environment is necessary to understand the behavior of companies. The company's reference environment, i.e., that part of the general context relevant to the achievement of company objectives, consists of the meso context, which includes the company's relationship networks with customers, suppliers, intermediaries, and competitors, and the macro environment.

The reference environment plays a very important role in the accumulation of knowledge and in the development of relationships, which constitute the fundamental resources of a company. For example, relationships with customers or suppliers develop in the environment and it is there that the most important learning processes take place. The type and quality of the company's fundamental resources therefore depend on the quality of the context, which is closely connected to the generation of value.

These relationships, which could once be defined as relatively simple, have today become extremely complex and even the traditional distinctions between the players operating within the markets and the competitive arena are blurring, making it very difficult to understand the phenomena through a stylization and a simplification.

In reality, as we know, the environment does not become more or less complex in itself, but becomes so in relation to whoever observes it and interacts with it. So, when we say that there is a complexification of the context, in reality we are talking about a complexification of the company which, becoming more and more complex, can no longer have simple relationships with the environment itself.

It is necessary to accept and face the element of complexity that has become a fundamental characteristic of the company and of the context in which it operates. Mazzoni therefore adopts the perspective of complexity to address the study of micro, meso, and macroeconomic relationships.

The explosion of the variety of market products, customers, competitors, suppliers, technologies, processes, products, environments, accompanied by the speed of change, market globalization, market instability, explosion of new technologies, has in fact pushed the level of complexity to such an extent that the recipes of the past have become useless, if not completely misleading.

Fortunately, the science of the last century has introduced new ideas on reality and new philosophical conceptions, which are transforming our knowledge of the world and our idea of reality, formed by centuries of science and philosophy. For millennia we have been used to certainties based on our senses and reasoning. We have always been immersed in the idea that reality is certain and we have been dominated by theories on the perfect functioning of the world. We grew up with ideas based on our reasoning, fueled by the extraordinary results and advances that science has given us in the seventeenth, eighteenth, and nineteenth centuries, in the fields of physics, biology, chemistry, medicine, politics and economics.

However, at the beginning of the last century, in the 1920s and 1930s, something shocking and extraordinary happened in science: Heisenberg introduced the uncertainty principle, Einstein proposed the theory of unified fields, Lamaître advanced the theory of the expansion of the universe, there was the birth of quantum theory. And just as Galilean and Newtonian physics gave us a new way of understanding the world, so this century's new physics and modern science are changing our perception of the world once again. And all fields of knowledge have been pervaded by these new conceptions of reality: philosophy, mathematics, cybernetics, chemistry, biology, sociology and, finally, economics.

Some principles have been introduced into science that have revolutionized our ideas about reality, and above all they have introduced the idea that reality cannot be known, that it cannot be predicted, that the future is not determined and, even more important, the fundamental idea that we do not observe the world, but we participate in it. Reality is not external to what we do and the world is the result of the interaction between our action and what exists in itself. Clelia Mazzoni draws on the evolution of scientific thought of the last century, particularly in the field of biological and social studies, brought about above all by Maturana and Varela and by Luhmann, to develop her reflections on the relationship between the company and the environment.

Starting from this robust body of theory, Clelia Mazzoni clarifies that the complexity of micro, meso and macro relationships plays an important role in the difficulty of establishing boundaries between different, increasingly permeable and unstable systems. There are numerous areas of overlap and close interaction between a business and its network, between a business and its suppliers, customers, and sometimes even competitors. The only solution that seems appropriate for a definition of boundaries, where they seem increasingly evanescent, is to assume an internal point of view of the actor whose boundaries are to be established.

The boundaries of a system can only be defined by the system itself. Each company defines what its boundaries are, and this definition can be different and sometimes even incompatible with that of another system which in turn establishes its boundaries. The only way to deal with complexity is to take different perspectives depending on the systems to be examined and to accept the apparent contradiction that emerges. The boundaries of a system can never be established externally, only from an internal perspective. And there is no objective point of view to address the issue.

Assuming the right perspective does not eliminate the complexity, but it clarifies that the company must accept this complexity, with the awareness that its way of defining itself and of defining its identity is never consistent with that of customers, suppliers, competitors, and that the different perspectives of the various players must coexist. Only the company capable of understanding the nature of this complexity and of accepting the coexistence of different perspectives can successfully play its role.

To address this complexity, Chiara Mazzoni examines micro, meso, and macro relationships from the perspective of complex systems. This perspective overcomes the dichotomy between closure and opening of systems in relations with the environment. The first must be understood as the need to generate the identity of the system through reference to itself, the second as the ability to draw energy from the environment to face complexity. Starting from this contemporary existence of closure and openness, it is possible to understand the relationships between social systems, therefore the growing complexity of the company and of the context.

Here Clelia Mazzoni tackles the point, never fully resolved on a theoretical level, of the relationship between the individual and the company. Both are systems, different from each other, which nonetheless have a relationship, to use Luhmann's words, of "interprenetration," that is, in which each participates in the constitution of the other. This means that each system makes an essential contribution to the existence of the other, while not being part of it. This apparent contradiction depends on the fact that each system sees the other as a constituent part, but sees itself as independent of the other. This happens because both systems agree to make certain fundamental elements available to the other, while maintaining autonomy.

Once the complexity relationships between firm and context have been defined, it is inevitable to conclude that the firm is an autopoietic system, the closure of which defines the environment of the firm itself. Therefore, there are no longer identical markets, sectors, networks, areas for all companies, but there is a context that each company defines in a totally autonomous way. Likewise, the boundaries between companies are very clear when you take the perspective of one of them, but become completely blurred when you take an outside point of view. From the latter perspective, in fact, it becomes very difficult, if not impossible, to be able to clearly define the boundaries and environments of organizations.

The topic, not addressed in this work by Clelia Mazzoni, but which in my opinion constitutes its inevitable consequence, is how a company must operate in a context of growing internal and external complexity. The answer is that a system can figure out how to relate to an environment it perceives as more complex, only through exploration. Exploring simply means accepting that the given interpretation of the context can only be provisional, because it depends neither on the characteristics of the latter nor on those of the company, but depends on both at the same time. This means that the only way for a company to deal with complexity is to accept its interpretations as provisional and act to try to make these interpretations, if not true, at least feasible and possibly functional for the company itself.

From this point of view, the ability to make mistakes and to learn, and the ability to tolerate the presence of errors within the organization, indeed to consider the latter as necessary, is the truly essential element for existence in a context of complexity. But this is another chapter, of which today's managerial literature is perhaps slowly becoming aware.

In summary, Clelia Mazzoni's work is one of the rare contributions in the field of economic and business literature that considers the need to read the relationship between the company and its context from the perspective of what is defined as the Economics of Complexity. It's not an easy job, because the theme of the relationship between system and context is not simple. Clelia knows how to make understandable a theme that few are able to deal with lucidity and competence. This is an excellent work, which every scholar of business economics should know, in order to understand the complex relationships between the company and its environment.

Bocconi University
Milan, Italy

Salvatore Vicari

Contents

List of Figures

1
Introduction

Abstract This study aims to analyze the relationship between the firm, traditionally a micro unit of economic studies, and the meso and macroeconomic contexts to which it consistently relates, with particular reference to industries and markets.

As an initial approximation, we define the industry as all companies that produce goods that are similar (delimitation based on supply) or substitutable among them (delimitation based on demand). Markets will be defined as the places of exchange where the company acquires the factors of production (labor market, supply of raw materials, services and technology market, and financial market) or sells its products/services (distribution and consumer market).

As a matter of fact in phenomenal reality, the relationships between the company, sector, and markets are quite complex, presenting themselves in ways that are ambiguous, often nuanced, almost always fluid, and continuously changing. Therefore we felt the need to study micro, meso, and macroeconomic relations within a context called the *Economics of Complexity*. This expression is intended to jointly consider an objective modification of the objects of study and a change in the method of analysis, a different epistemological approach in dealing with research topics.

Complexity is a transversal methodological instance: theories on complexity have developed in parallel and independently within multiple disciplinary domains of contemporary scientific research.

C. Mazzoni, *Firms, Industries, Markets*, https://doi.org/10.1007/978-3-031-59823-4_1

Keywords Micro, meso and macro relationships in Economics • Micro, meso and macro relationships within a simplified interpretation • Micro, meso and macro relationships in current phenomenology • The *Economics of Complexity* • From classical science to the epistemology of complexity

1.1 Micro, Meso, and Macro Relationships in Economics

This study aims to analyze the relationship between the firm, traditionally a micro unit of economic studies, and the meso[1] and macroeconomic contexts to which it consistently relates, with particular reference to industries and markets.

The premise of the entire project lies in the conviction that to understand firms' phenomena (the microeconomic dimension), examining in depth the relationships between the company and the *task environment* (the meso and macroeconomic context closest to it) is essential. To refer to the macroenvironment of closest relevance to the company, we will use the term task environment with reference to the original meaning by Dill (1958)[2] and in the subsequent meaning by Newell and Simon (1972).[3] This term indicates the part of the environment

[1] The term mesoeconomics is generally used to identify intermediate units ideally placed between microeconomic agents (typically, in management studies, firms) and macroeconomic contexts (traditionally represented by aggregate supply and demand). On the subject, see, among others, Dopfer et al. (2004) and Mann (2011). Therefore, industries, some regional economies, and in a broader sense, industrial districts and business networks can be considered mesoeconomic units.

[2] "I have denoted the part of the total environment of management, which was potentially relevant to goal setting and goal attainment, as the task environment" (Dill, 1958, p. 410).

[3] "The term *task environment*, as we shall use it, refers to an environment coupled with a goal, problem, or task—the one for which the motivation of the subject is assumed. It is the task that defines a point of view about an environment, and that, in fact, allows an environment to be delimited" (Newell & Simon, 1972, p. 55).

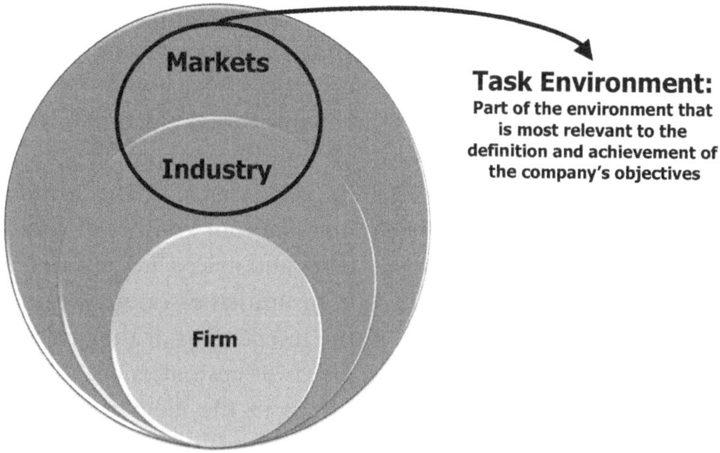

Fig. 1.1 Study units

most relevant to the definition and achievement of the company's objectives[4] (Fig. 1.1).

The interaction between the firms and their reference environments explains many entrepreneurial dynamics and allows us to investigate their specificities and relative performances. The conditions of the task environment influence the company's behaviors, decision-making rationality, and structures. Reciprocally, the movements of microeconomic units contribute to defining environmental scenarios and allow studying the changes that take place in industries and markets. Possessing a theoretical perspective[5] that enables interpreting this relation (and giving it meaning) is essential for those who study or manage companies.

Understanding the relationships between the company and task environment becomes even more relevant in a perspective wherein the value of intangible resources is emphasized (company reputation, trust on the

[4] During the work, the expressions "task environment," "reference environment," "reference context," "reference macroaggregates," "reference macrocontext," and "environmental context" will be used synonymously.

[5] As will be specified later, the choice of the expression "theoretical perspective" responds to the need to indicate something more general than a theory or a model; rather, it refers to a structure that generates theories or scientific models.

part of customers and stakeholders in general, aptitude for generating innovation, competence of human resources, organizational and technological know-how, and communication skills). If we admit that the production of value is fed more by the intangible content incorporated in the goods exchanged than by the physical transformation of raw materials into artifacts and if we agree that the production of these intangible resources is mainly linked to the accumulation of knowledge and development of relationships, the micro, meso, and macro link takes on a new and more profound meaning. In fact, in numerous cases, learning processes (knowledge) are generated in the interactions of the firm with its task environment. For example, the needs of customers are explored or technological know-how is acquired. It is in the meso and macroeconomic context that a large part of the relationships is produced (agreements with suppliers, relationships with stakeholders, cooperation agreements, consumer loyalty). In this sense, the generation of intangible resources is possible mainly in consideration of an external reference context: knowledge and relationships are produced in the relations with this context which are then reworked and made unique by the company's internal management. In the economy of intangible resources, the micro, meso, and macro relationship is significant from another point of view: it is in the task environment that a company with a high content of intangible value is appreciated and recognized as the bearer of differential qualities. Without an external evaluation, it would be impossible to judge the differences between products and/or services and between the companies themselves.

Consequently, the relationship with the reference context co-generates resources on the one hand, while on the other, it legitimizes the diversity and uniqueness of the mix contained in the products/services offered. Delving into the sense of the relationship between the firm and its task environment is relevant to understanding the genesis of learning processes, construction of the network of relationships, and ways of generating and distributing value.

It was decided to give the work a theoretical–interpretative approach as opposed to a normative one because the work does not aspire, if not indirectly, to provide business/managerial behavior models. The regulatory intent is consequential insofar as a good interpretative framework provides scholars, managers, and entrepreneurs with a useful interpretation to guide their decision-making processes. The awareness, for example, of a scenario characterized by high degrees of complexity and the consequent perception of being unable to dominate the micro, meso, and macro relationship in the economy through deterministic schemes helps the entrepreneur and manager to control the stress and frustration produced by this situation. Possessing an upstream vision (a meta-vision) that enriches the ability to interpret phenomena without necessarily forcing them into simplistic models of explanation favors a mental attitude and a decision-making rationality in consonance with the actual possibilities of maneuvering and control.

In this work, the analysis of the interaction between firm and task environment borrows concepts from different disciplines. This multidisciplinarity is favored by the points of contact of the firm-task environment relationships with multiple fields of knowledge. The company is, in fact, at the crossroads of a relationships' network that favor the mutual contamination of theoretical approaches and different languages: as a social organization (with an exceptional possibility of interaction with sociological and psychological disciplines), with regard to its technical knowledge (use of engineering and physical or computer skills in the company), as an engine of the economic system (influence of entrepreneurial behaviors on economic and political scenarios), and as a receiver and translator of legal–regulatory systems.

For some time, Management has limited its disciplinary domain by drawing a very clear boundary line between the micro, meso, and macroeconomic dimensions. This was under the assumption that the privileged object of study (precisely, the company) could be isolated while concentrating attention exclusively on it. The evidence of the phenomenical reality suggests an opportunity to modify this route and seek a theoretical perspective that connects micro, meso, and macroeconomics in a dialectic of continuous, reciprocal references by not only definitively legitimizing the conversation of Management with disciplines sensitive to economic contexts by their nature (Microecomics, Macroeconomics, Political Economy, and Industrial Organization) but also using contaminations that come from other scientific circuits. In this sense, the reflection on micro, meso, and macroeconomic relations cannot fail to make use of the enrichments that come from various disciplinary fields. In this work, we felt the need to deviate from the more consolidated paths of management scholars and approach also concepts as in Sociology, Cybernetics, Biology, and Chemistry. Needless to say, this journey was undertaken with the humility and caution of those who approach notions and languages, which in some cases are very far from their cultural background and, therefore, with the impossibility of a detailed study that is necessary for a complete analysis of the issues being addressed. Nevertheless, recognizing that the paths taken in our disciplines are very close to those being explored in other fields of knowledge is important. These paths should not remain parallel; rather, they should intersect to openly discuss how to continue the journey.

1.2 Micro, Meso, and Macro Relationships Within a Simplified Interpretation

The objects of study identified for the analysis proposed below are the firm, industries, and markets.

As mentioned, we will refer to the firm as the micro unit of our discussion, whereas we will be using the industry and markets to lead us back to the meso and macro objects of interest. As an initial approximation, we can define the industry as all companies that produce goods that are similar (delimitation based on supply) or substitutable among them (delimitation based on demand). Markets will be defined as the places of exchange where the company acquires the factors of production (labor market, supply of raw materials, services and technology market, and financial market) or sells its products/services (distribution and consumer market).

This is a simplified approach, which nonetheless is necessary to initiate the analysis. As we will see, this analysis will become much more complex as we look at this relation from different perspectives using distinctive theoretical approaches.

In this initial hypothesis, the interpretation of the firm–industry–markets links takes place with a simplified perspective, which we could define as linear according to a scheme of essential relationships, wherein objects are clearly defined and relationships are clearly determinable.

The linearity of these links is exemplified in Fig. 1.2.

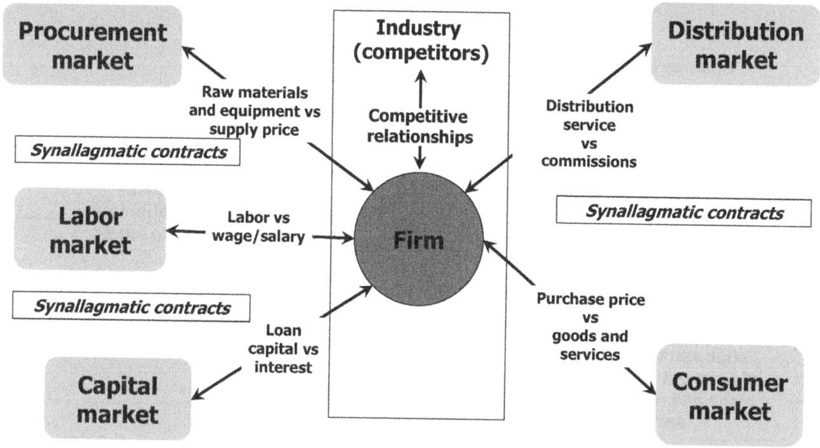

Fig. 1.2 Linear micro, meso, and macro relations: Well-defined boundaries and clearly determinable relationships

Boundaries are identified as follows: the *firm* as an element of analysis is clearly recognizable with respect to other companies and the environmental context with which it relates; the *industry* is easily distinguishable as a reference unit, and its margins are immediately traceable; the same can be said for the *markets* where transactions take place. Relationships are defined on the basis of competition (among firms in the sector) or on the basis of exchange (between the firm and markets). Within an industry, the mutual consideration of companies is based on a pattern of competition, whereas in the markets, the relationships are synallagmatic: the company receives capital in exchange for interest; workforce in exchange for wages; raw materials, technologies, and services in exchange for supply price; and distribution services in exchange for commissions. The company also sells the produced goods and/or services in the consumer market in exchange for a payment for their sale.

1.3 Micro, Meso, and Macro Relationships in Current Phenomenology

In phenomenical reality, the relationships between the company, sector, and markets are quite complex, presenting themselves in ways that are

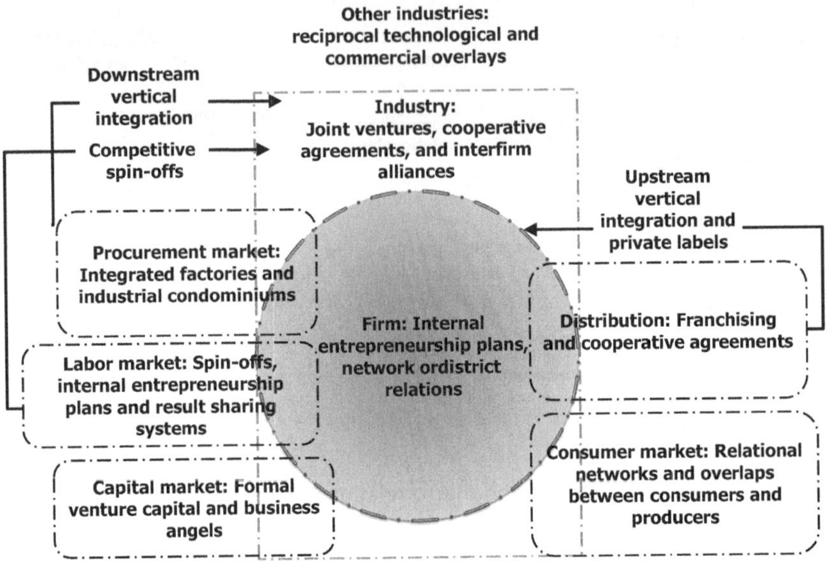

Fig. 1.3 Micro, meso, and macro relations in the current phenomenology: Permeable boundaries and varying relationships

ambiguous, often nuanced, almost always fluid, and continuously changing. We tried to reproduce them in Fig. 1.3.

We can determine the definition of an *industry* by trying to understand what it contains and its boundary with other sectors. In Fig. 1.2 we had used a parameter of industry delimitation based on supply (… companies that produce similar goods belong to the same sector …) or demand (… goods considered substitutable …). These criteria do not appear suitable to permanently and noncontingently represent the phenomena recorded today in the original sectoral space.

What is the system for defining two similar goods? For a long time, the product's classification criterion was used as a demarcation element, which implicitly referred to a common technological core (this is why the principle is identified as aggregative with respect to similarities on the supply side). Currently, the technological parameter provides poor stability in defining the industry, as the same technologies are used for particularly different applications and, conversely, considering the technological overlaps within the same production. For example, to which sector does a company such as Amazon, where various production and service technologies coexist, belong? Is it part of the Commercial Distribution, Logistics, or Information and Communication Technology? It is probably a small part of each of these sectors but not exclusive to any. Is there a new sector in which similar companies can be placed on the technological front? What persistence could we attribute to a new delimitation that was created ad hoc?

Attempting to establish a dividing line is rather difficult, particularly in areas between sectors that are originally different but strongly affected by alliances, common development projects, technological convergence, and integrated research. We are not referring to traditional diversification and integration strategies, which nevertheless generate interesting phenomena of sectoral interdependence, but to recent phenomena of cross-border and cross-sectoral innovation. The digital economy and use of Artificial Intelligence (AI) have led, for example, to the convergence of different technologies and to the collision of industries that were originally distinct, thereby generating new market areas that are difficult to identify with *a priori* criteria.

In fact, new technologies are often closely interrelated to the extent that developing a new application requires the convergence of several different branches of scientific knowledge and technologies; in some industries—such as Data Transmission, Optical Fibers, Artificial Intelligence, and Biotechnologies—companies cannot oversee a single technological boundary to control the evolution of the competitive environment (Vicari & Bertoli, 2000, p. 178).

Within the same sector, it does not help us to take up the reference criterion that provides for companies producing goods considered substitutable by consumers (in this sense, the principle is considered discriminatory from the demand perspective), even if they come from different technological environments. In pursuing this path, we find surprising substitution phenomena within the same original sectoral space to the point that today, a cotton towel (textile technology) is in competition with a roll of absorbent paper (paper converting) and an electrical machine that emits hot air (consumer electronics) because they all have the specific function of drying an individual's hands. How far can this road take us? How can we reconstruct a stable meso-aggregate wherein forms of affinities not dictated by specific contingencies can be found? In fact, the theorists of imperfect markets (through the cross elasticity between different goods), in defining the sector as a set of companies that produce "fairly good substitutes" (Chamberlin, 1937, p. 567), had envisaged some possibility of breaking up predefined products or services industries. Yet, they undoubtedly did not have the contemporary substitution phenomena in mind.

All this has led to the search for new units of measurement (e.g., strategic business area) that break the traditional sectoral limits and propose a customization of the boundaries according to the needs of the analysis.

In the description of the simplified relations in Fig. 1.2, we also stated that the industry includes enterprises competing against each other (the competitive criterion somewhat summarizes those based on demand and those based on supply). Currently, however, business convergence systems, such as networks and districts, go hand in hand and/or overlap with traditional competition; the development of joint ventures and cooperative agreements in general between potentially competing enterprises does not leave much room for a description based exclusively on competitive criteria. It is difficult to maintain that the sector comprises competing companies because within spaces that are quite similar to the original sectors, there are companies that, in addition to competing, cooperate to improve individual and organizational learning and create new knowledge.

Moreover, phenomena such as networks and districts lead to a question that is even more difficult to answer. Do these aggregates belong to the meso dimension (e.g., they are a portion of the sector), or are they representative of the micro dimension (they take the place of the company we traditionally refer to)? One peculiarity of studies on entrepreneurial networks is precisely that of giving a renewed identity to the mesoeconomic dimension.

Within the outline of Fig. 1.3, there are also doubts regarding the identifiability of the *firm* as a distinct object from other companies and from its reference macroaggregates. In a network–enterprise or in a network of enterprises, what is the object of our study? The individual enterprise or the system generated by mutual interdependencies?

In modular networks (composed of numerous differentiated modules that can be recombined), the completion of the process occurs only through the joint activity of operators who play complementary roles (Rullani, 2004, pp. 126–127):

- *Specialists* focus on a very limited scope and build standard elementary components that can be used by a multiplicity of users.
- By recombining the base modules provided by specialists from time to time, *systems analysts* activate complex product or service architectures.
- *Connectors* provide the first two with logistical, communication, and warranty services.
- *Meta-organizers* design networks and define their operating methods.

Besides, each of these operators can also work within differentiated networks.

Where do we trace the boundaries of a company in a modular system such as the one described above? Is the company the overall system, or is it the single participant in the process?

Moreover, how do we define the boundaries of a company that develops Internal Corporate Venturing (ICV) initiatives[6] for the creation of new correlated businesses with their employees, thereby constituting new legally autonomous enterprises in some cases? Likewise, where are the boundaries when a new company is created from spin-off processes led by a parent company, which provides significant contributions to address the start-up and postentry phases? In these circumstances, does the original company contain the new company? How much of the knowledge and relationships (intangible, value-generating resources) of the original company did the new unit bring with it? Is it the new company that holds part of the parent company? In such circumstances, it is reasonable to ask whether when looking for the extremities of our micro object, we should refer to the parent company, the new company, or a combination of both. It probably depends on what we are focusing on, what we aspire to put in the foreground, and what we want to tone down in the

---

[6] For a review of the literature on ICV, see Hill and Georgoulas (2016).

background (this aspect of the choice of the observation point will be, as we will see, a recurring theme of this work).

Even the territoriality criterion, which, until a few decades ago, appeared binding in identifying the company because it was linked to the physical criteria (an industrial factory or a place of supply of the service) seems to have dissolved when the company is no longer associated with a factory, store, or bank office. The abandonment of the physical reference in the definition of boundaries (made possible by the evolution of organizations in a branched and sprawling sense and by the parallel digital revolution) went hand in hand with the spread of decontextualized companies, transnational networks, and virtual districts not connected to certain geographical areas but connected due to high-tech intangible services and infrastructures. In this sense, digital globalization is a phenomenon that also affects business models. Territoriality, albeit having made possible some aggregations based on affinities of entrepreneurial behavior and structure (small and medium-sized Italian enterprises, large US corporations) becomes a labile criterion for generating significant and stable taxonomies. Behavioral differences among companies depend less on geographical differences and increasingly on the growing complexity and articulation of the environment, which allows and generates the coexistence of different entrepreneurial formulas.

The difficulty of separately identifying the study objects also concerns the third element that we have considered, namely, *markets*. According to the simplified interpretation used in Fig. 1.2, they represent places of trade, where the company acquires the inputs needed and markets its products and/or services. Today, the actors of these exchanges enter in the processes of value generation in a more direct but less codifiable manner. Think of what is happening in the *market of supply*. Traditionally, it was a transactional environment for the acquisition of materials and services necessary for production. Today, it is more closely, but not linearly, connected and associated to the management of the supply chain through the most varied formulas that go from outsourcing to networks, from integrated factories to districts, from industrial condominiums to affiliations along the supply chains.

Can we, in the presence of these phenomena, still talk of the supply market as a simple place of exchange? How much of the supply mechanism becomes part of the original definition of enterprise? In integrated factories, industrial condominiums, or networks along the supply chain, where does the company end and where does the supply market begin?

Many doubts also arise in the study of the company's relationship with the *labor market* and in the attempt to define the boundaries between the two. We need to ask whether employees are workers, external to the company and linked to the organization only by a synallagmatic contract that establishes the terms of the transaction (work against salary/wage), or if the human resources are part of the company because they actively contribute to the value production process and are coauthors of the possible success of the entrepreneurial action. In some cases, there is significant difficulty in determining whether employees are the counterparty of a transactional act (and therefore belong to a market with which the company exchanges resources) or whether they are internal to the company system (an element of the micro reference unit). This happens when the transactional synallagma, originally determined by performance and counter-performance, is transformed into a more articulated contract wherein the worker, through internal entrepreneurship initiatives or the management of guided spin-offs, is led to participate in the governance processes of the organization. Literature on the possibility of involving human resources in the management and creation of systems with widespread entrepreneurship testifies to the hybridization of the figure of the worker who, in many cases, far from being only the counterpart of an exchange, shares a portion of the entrepreneurial risk and possible benefits of successful performance. Where do we place workers willing to link their remuneration to the results of management or the internal entrepreneur who takes charge of launching a new product or managing a new business? Do they have to be part of the labor market or of the enterprise?

Even in the *financial market,* we find examples that are not easily explained by the traditional logic of the transaction. When capital providers become part of the company's management by introducing formulas, such as merchant banking or formal venture capital, are we in the presence of operators external to the company or do they, even if for a limited time, become an integral part of the company? The same question arises where multiple individuals participate with ideas and proposals on equity crowdfunding platforms. The boundary line between investor and entrepreneur is even more blurred in the presence of business angels, who intervene in decision-making processes even more than formal venture capitalists. Moreover, business angels, often coming from industrial experiences similar to those they finance, are also (or have been) in some way a part of the company's reference sector. If we were to embrace a simplified reading of micro, meso, and macro relationships such as that described in Fig. 1.2, we would find ourselves faced with the paradox that a certain operator (the business angel) is present in the market (as an investor and, therefore, counterparty of a transactional act), the company (as a participant in the strategic choices of the latter), and the industry (as an entrepreneur or ex-entrepreneur of the same branch).

Additionally, the collision phenomena between companies and distribution make it increasingly difficult to look at the *distribution market* as a place of exchange characterized by simple and linear transactions. In a phenomenon such as franchising, where does the industrial enterprise end and where does the commercial enterprise begin? By adding value to it, are the many points of sale of a franchise chain an extension of the original company to some extent? With respect to the franchisor, who imprints the creation of franchisee companies (transferring not only the products and/or services to be distributed but also the know-how, image, brand, and all the distinctive signs), to what extent is it part of the distribution chains? How do we frame partnership agreements and collaborative formulas between industrial companies and distribution, which consolidate the vertical marketing channels, where a system of cooperative and competitive relationships completely redefines the role of the commercial enterprise? How do we evaluate the phenomena of affirmation of private labels such that some large-scale retail distribution companies are present in the distribution market, sector (as competitors), and vertical chain of purchase (when they buy the products unlabeled by the industry-branded producers) at the same time?

Even the *consumer market*, traditionally a terminal receiver of upstream production activity, today enters into the coproduction of value. The digital transformation, the development of relational marketing and marketing networks, push the producers and distributors to carry out some of the activities at the consumer level through the codesign of customized products or by providing the consumer with a technical and linguistic capacity that facilitates the adoption of products/services with many possibilities of use. In this circumstance as well, the spread of the Internet and of new digital technologies has given visibility and (paradoxically) physicalized the phenomenon: an online forum is coproduced owing to the participation of a large number of users; a social community is fed because new users make contributions to a potentially infinite electronic archive where animators have made available only the basic technology; today customers design their own online version of the product or service that they wish to purchase.

Therefore, the original conceptualizations of the enterprise, industry, and market lose their explanatory capacity in the division of the micro space from the meso and macro ones. In these cases, they are no longer complementary domains; rather, they overlap and penetrate each other.

1.4 The *Economics of Complexity*

Defining complexity is not easy. To try to share the concept of complexity, we primarily referenced a series of conversations on the subject between Giorgio Parisi, winner of the 2021 Nobel Prize for Physics for his studies on complex systems, and Mauro Ceruti, a philosopher of science who has been dealing with the epistemology of complexity for many decades.[7] These conversations stress the difficulty of defining complexity. To this end, Ceruti proposes considering the etymology of the word. The root of the Latin verb *plectere* (intertwine), preceded by the preposition *cum*, returns the meaning of several elements, "intertwined together" and "intertwined several times," that is, a plurality of components that nevertheless determines something unitary. This multiplicity in unity allows descriptions at different levels from that of single components to intermediate stages up to the description of the higher level and to observe a

[7] Parisi and Ceruti (2013) https://www.complexityinstitute.it/.

mutual influence of the events that occur at different levels of the system. Parisi recalls that many different definitions of complexity were given, most of which refer to the difference between "complex" and "complicated":

> In a complicated world, the various elements that make up the system maintain a degree of independence from one another. Thus, removing one such element (which reduces the level of complication) does not fundamentally alter the system's behavior apart from that which directly results from the piece that was removed. Complexity arises when the dependencies among the elements become important. In such a system, removing one such element destroys system behavior to an extent that goes well beyond what is embodied by the particular element that is removed…When a scientist faces a complicated world, traditional tools that rely on reducing the system to its atomic elements allow us to gain insight. Unfortunately, using these same tools to understand complex worlds fails, because it becomes impossible to reduce the system without killing it. (Miller & Page, 2007, pp. 9–10)

The thesis of the scientific rationality of the 1700s and 1800s implied the predictability of future events on the basis of scientific theories, which were defined as such precisely on the basis of their ability to pre-establish what would happen in later eras. In complex systems, this predictability of future states is not detectable. The variety and variability[8] of the company's relationships with the meso and macroeconomic contexts, for example, make it very difficult to predict the result of the relationships themselves because in complex systems, the ability to adapt and coevolve over time with respect to environmental circumstances makes changes absolutely contingent. By introducing the temporal dimension, we come to the observation of systems that have evolved in a certain way but could have had numerous other outcomes that could even be very different from what has actually been achieved. Such a possible evolution cannot

[8] In the various, in many cases implicit, proposals for measuring complexity, the concepts of variety and variability are often used, meaning the number of possible cases (variety) and their modification in relation to spatiotemporal categories (variability).

be probabilistically studied. In the aforementioned dialogues, Parisi notes that the probability of, for example, vertebrates developing among all the species present 530 million years ago was very low. There were only very few species that presented the characteristics of vertebrates, and if those very few species had become extinct, today we would not have this type of life on earth.

Therefore, many questions are raised from a more in-depth reading of the economic relations among objects traditionally defined as micro, meso, and macro. We could say that this reading generates further doubt in the observer: is this complexity only linked to the greater articulation of the phenomena, or is it also a consequence of the adoption of a more multifaceted interpretative key? Have the objects of study (the firm, industry, and markets) and their mutual interconnections simply become more complex, or do the epistemological changes in progress compel us to use a lens that allows us to look at the same phenomena differently? In other words, is complexity a matter of modifying objective reality, or is it also a change in our approach, method of study, and epistemological statute?

With this question, we fully enter into the issue of complexity, which has involved many sciences and is now also engaging Management:

> As its basis, complexity thinking assumes that the world is comprised of a myriad elements that interact … So a complex system comprises many unique elements that interact in multiple ways. The elements themselves can change, learn, and adapt. The connections can change, loosen, and reform, and the boundaries of the system can also shift over time. (Boulton et al., 2015, p. 34)

Based on these premises, we felt the need to study micro, meso, and macroeconomic relations within a context called the *Economics of Complexity*.[9] This expression is intended to jointly consider an objective

[9] Even if the use of the concept of complexity in economic studies is at an early stage, there are several applications of theories on complexity in Economics, Finance, Public Policy, Management, and Organization. See, among others, Mitleton-Kelly (2003); Kirman (2004, 2016); Foster (2005); Grimm et al. (2005); Beinhocker (2006, 2013); Salzano and Colander (2007); Fontana (2010); Holt et al. (2011); Durlauf (2012); Dolphin and Nash (2012); Helbing and Kirman (2013); Arthur (2014); Boulton et al. (2015); Battiston et al. (2016); Heise (2017); Tain (2021).

modification of the objects of study (first of all, the company itself) and a change in the method of analysis, a different epistemological approach in dealing with research topics.[10] It is not easy to establish how the first element (change of economic reality) influenced the second element (methodological renewal) or how the opposite is true. Does the legitimacy of the study of complex phenomena, previously marginalized, derive from the abandoning of the universalist abstraction (Morin, 2007, p. 26) that forced us to an unjustified simplification of reality? What seems clear is that phenomenological and epistemological complexity go hand in hand, and it becomes difficult to face the study of phenomena, such as that of micro, meso, and macroeconomic relations, while leaving aside this assumption.

This approach obviously involves not only having a pluralism of epistemological statutes and therefore the lack of a single method for cognitive evolution in all fields of knowledge but also a re-evaluation of the organization of knowledge. A society founded on the departmentalization of knowledge risks not being sensitive to diversity outside and within. For this reason too, phenomenological complexity must necessarily be combined with the complexity of an epistemological nature because complexity is not only a property of the observed system but also of the observing system; it is in the nature of things as well as in the representations that we construct (Le Moigne, 2007, p. 74). In the *Economics of Complexity*, the intricacy of companies as objects of study grows along with the complexity used methodologically by those who scrutinize it. Simultaneously, the complexity of companies (and other operators involved in the micro, meso, and macro relationship) as subjects observing the increasingly complex external environment develops. In summary, the study of micro, meso, and macro relations must deal with the following issues:

- The complexity of companies as an object of study.
- The complexity of the reference environment of the companies.

[10] What emerges is that not only companies change continuously, as part of their evolutionary nature, but we, as observers, also change when we consider previous modes of representation as being unsatisfactory (Vicari, 2024, p. 5).

- The complexity of companies (and other operators acting within the relationship) in their capacity as actors interpreting the complexity of the external reality.
- The complexity in the evolution of Management and, in general, of socioeconomic disciplines.

The complexity of the company as an object of study and observant subject also entails the need for an evolved analysis methodology and a rethinking of the relationship between the observer and observed system.

Therefore, it being difficult to approach complexity through a preliminary explanation (Morin, 2007, p. 25), without denying its very nature, we will rather try to show how the *Economics of Complexity* fits into what is now recognized as a broader movement that, with different times and methods, involves many disciplines. In fact, some scholars from various disciplines have begun to examine the theories of complex systems in depth, coming together in a movement united by the common thread of "complexity" (Vicari, 2024, p. 10).

1.4.1 From Classical Science to the Epistemology of Complexity

Aristotelianism viewed the world as perfectly ordered. Deviations were interpreted as distortions from the ordinary state, and attempts were made to eliminate them. As early as the sixteenth century, astronomical and geographical discoveries began to insinuate some doubt about the supposed perfection of the world, but this was insufficient to develop a theory that predicted the *improbability of the normal* (Luhmann, 2016, p. 233). In the seventeenth century, René Descartes gave new meaning to the subjectivity of consciousness, linking certainty to the self-reference of the latter. Considering doubt as an essential methodological element, the only existence that could not be questioned was the conscience of the thinking and doubting individual. Starting from this as the sole factor of truth, Descartes developed a methodological theory based on the use of analysis and logical deduction and on the support of mathematics (Pheby, 1990, pp. 14–15). In the eighteenth century, Enlightenment ideas proliferated based on the replacement of the supernatural with the natural, on the exaltation of reason guided by experience, and on faith in the perfectibility of man. In the first half of the nineteenth century, Auguste Comte argued that there was a possibility of extending the model of the natural sciences to social sciences and sought the fundamental laws of human progress, which affirmed the new positive science. Positivism, which historically derives from the thought of Bacon and Descartes,[11] despite the diversity of its theoretical approaches,[12] spread the idea that a scientific methodology could also be used for the analysis of social phenomena and that "the society of man must be studied in the same scientific manner as the world of nature" (Coser, 2012, p. 3):

> René Descartes created the method of analytic thinking, which consists of breaking up complex phenomena into pieces to understand the behavior of the whole from the properties of its parts. (Capra, 1997, p. 19)

At the beginning of the twentieth century, "logical positivism" took root, which aspired to give philosophical bases to the scientific method. This current of thought, which had a dominant position in the Philosophy of Science at the beginning of the century, stimulated the idea that even in Economics, there could be objective formulations similar to those of experimental sciences and suggested the distinction between normative and positive economics (Landreth & Colander, 1994, p. 11). In particular, Friedman defined positive economics as "a system of generalisations that can be used to make correct predictions about the consequences of any change in circumstances. Its performance is to be judged by the precision, scope, and conformity of the predictions it yields" (Friedman cited in Pheby, 1990, p. 85).

In more recent times, theoretical approaches based on the empirical confirmation of general laws have also begun to falter in natural sciences,

---

[11] The objectives of Bacon and Descartes were similar, although the instruments used were opposite because Bacon had an approach connected to the inductive method, whereas Descartes theorized the validity of deductive reasoning. On the subject of deductivism and inductivism, with particular reference to Economics, see Pheby (1990, pp. 1–21).

[12] Positivism has taken on different connotations in France (Comte), England (Spencer), and Germany (Moleshott, Vogt, Buchner).

the cradle of experimental methodology. Einsteinian physics, for example, is a construction based essentially on a conceptual intuition, which has received experimental confirmations only after the formulation of the theory itself. Heisenberg's uncertainty principle emphasizes the impossibility of exactly measuring the effects of a phenomenon owing to the intervention of external observation, thereby asserting that the same circumstance of simultaneously calculating the position and speed of a moving particle conditions its motion, making the measurement itself imprecise.

At the same time, we have begun to think about the real possibilities of checking the truthfulness of the hypotheses. Gödel's theorem, the fundamental theorem of logic, states that within a formal system with a complexity at least equal to that of arithmetic, some assertions are neither demonstrable nor falsifiable. In fact, to carry out this demonstration, it would be necessary to resort to a broader conceptual system that includes the first, a third that includes the second, and so on. The Halting problem formulated by Turing has shown that there is no procedure capable of establishing the correctness of another procedure, so, for example, a software will always host a certain number of bugs regardless of how many verification tests have been previously carried out.

Faced with the deterministic conceptions of classical science, in different disciplines, the way has been opened to reflections that consider the dynamic interdependencies between events, impossibility of analytical decomposition of phenomena, circular effects of feedback for which outputs are transformed into inputs in successive cycles, organization of elementary components into composite structures, impossibility of predicting future states connected to uncertainty, or spatiotemporal indetermination of the circumstances of becoming. Theories on complexity have developed in parallel and independently within multiple disciplinary domains of contemporary scientific research. In this sense, complexity is a transversal methodological instance with respect to natural sciences, social sciences, and humanistic culture. Hereinafter, we will mention some particularly significant aspects of the theories that, in different disciplines, have considered complex events to give a sense of the scope and longitudinality of the phenomenon and without, of course, any claim of exhaustiveness and completeness.

If we were to identify a precise moment of initiation of organized reflections on complexity, we could go back to March 1946, the date of the first meeting of what later became known as Macy Conferences, wherein the foundations of cybernetics and complex thought were implemented:

> The conceptual framework of cybernetics was developed in a series of legendary meetings in New York City, known as the Macy Conferences. These meetings—especially the first one in 1949—were extremely stimulating, bringing together a unique group of highly creative people who engaged in intense interdisciplinary dialogues to explore new ideas and ways of thinking. The participants fell into two core groups. The first formed around the original cyberneticists and consisted of mathematicians, engineers, and neuroscientists. The other group consisted of scientists from the humanities who clustered around Gregory Bateson and Margaret Mead. From the first meeting on, the cyberneticists made great efforts to bridge the academic gap between themselves and the humanities. (Capra, 1997, pp. 52–53)[13]

Mathematics was one of the first disciplines touched upon by the themes of complexity. English mathematician George Boole used operators with binary states (on/off, yes/no, 1/0) in the nineteenth century, thereby inventing symbolic logic called Boolean algebra (Capra, 1997, p. 195), which is the basis of computers. The nodes of a Boolean network can be connected with each other such that the future state of each of them depends on the present state of the others according to a systematic rule.[14] Therefore, a condition of interdependence is established between the operators from which the future condition of the network originates. This sequence of events generates cycles, which in some cases tend to repeat a succession of configurations (limit cycles). Von Neumann and Turing developed these concepts wherein the future states of the parts

[13] The Macy Conferences were characterized by the personality and different conceptions of two great intellectuals: John von Neumann (who first formulated the game theory based on the analysis of interdependent behaviors) and Norbert Wiener (mathematician and philosopher).

[14] Assuming, for example, that we have three bulbs that can assume the on or off state, let us suppose that each bulb turns on at time $t + 1$, if at time t both other bulbs were on. It follows that the configuration of the network at time $t + 1$ depends on the configuration of the network at time t.

depend not only on the state of the neighboring elements but also on the very distant ones. In these networks, the succession of states can generate chaotic patterns and ordered sequences.

Interconnection, interdependence, and the consequent generation of systems that oscillate between chaos and order are likely to help understand the complexity that characterizes systems such as enterprises, industries, markets, and their mutual relationships. The characteristics recalled are recurrent in the mathematics of complexity, mathematics considered more qualitative than quantitative, which privileges relationships and not objects and allows nonlinear phenomena to be treated without resorting to linear approximations. Chaos theories have arisen in this environment through which it is observed that apparently disordered forms can hide mechanisms that are not random. Chaotic behavior is not an accidental, completely irregular motion, although it is not possible to make accurate quantitative forecasts on it, but only of a qualitative nature. One of the reasons that makes long-term forecasts in a chaotic system difficult is the extreme sensitivity to initial conditions such that chain effects and distinctive trajectories can develop from almost coincident starting points. Additionally, the propagation of repeated and/or amplifying effects from these conditions means that very small changes in the initial state of chaotic systems generate far-reaching effects with the passage of time. This phenomenon is known as the *butterfly effect paradox*, highlighted by meteorologist Edward Lorenz, with which it is jokingly argued that the wing beat of a butterfly in Brazil can cause a tornado in Texas in a month (Lorenz, 1972).

Another topic emerging in Mathematics and rich in ideas for our discussion of complexity is the geometry of fractals, where we define a fractal as a fragmented geometric form whose parts are almost similar to the whole. Although irregular and complex, fractals can be generated by the mechanical repetition of very simple algorithms. As seen in Figs. 1.4 and 1.5 (in which two of the most famous fractals are represented, namely, Koch's Flake and the Mandelbrot set), the formation of a fractal occurs by repeating a basic geometric sign an infinite number of times, even a very trivial one, with a final effect that is, *vice versa*, highly sophisticated.

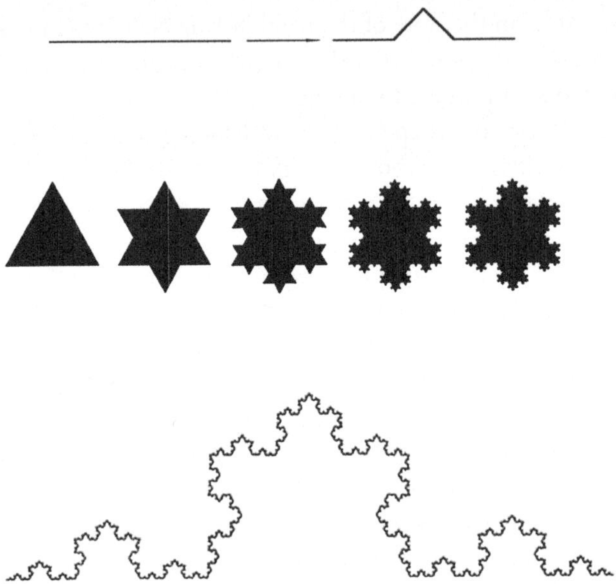

Fig. 1.4 Koch snowflakes. (Source: Capra (1997, pp. 138–139))

The basic idea of fractal geometry is that some forms in nature, such as clouds (Capra, 1997, p. 136), cannot be described with traditional geometry and require a more complex coding mechanism.

Fuzzy logic is a part of the same line of thought. It overcomes the dichotomy between true and false to admit, with the mathematics of fuzzy sets theory, that there may be phenomena that take on polyvalent values with gradation between the highest degree of falsehood and absolute truth.

One of the most advanced products of complex thought, as has already been mentioned, is *Cybernetics*. It is a discipline born from a fertile interaction between Biology, Mathematics, Physics, and Engineering and has seen the contribution of scientists such as Ross Ashby, Norbert Wiener, Heinz von Foerster, and Claude Shannon:

> Cybernetics was defined by Wiener as "the science of control and communication in the animal and the machine"… It takes as its subject-matter the domain of "all possible machines" and is only secondarily interested if informed that some of them have not yet been made, either by Man or by

Fig. 1.5 Mandelbrot set. (Source: Peitgen and Richter (1986, p. 22))

> Nature … The second peculiar virtue of cybernetics is that it offers a method for the scientific treatment of the system in which complexity is outstanding and too important to be ignored. Such systems are, as we well know, only too common in the biological world! In the simpler systems, the methods of cybernetics sometimes show no obvious advantage over those that have long been known. It is chiefly when the systems become complex that the new methods reveal their power. (Ashby, 2015, pp. 1–5)

The definition of the abstract machine, that is, the identification of the traits suitable for defining an apparatus, regardless of its actual concretization, is attributed to Alan Turing, who devised the so-called Turing machine, in which each state is defined by its previous internal state as well as by the previous state of the environment. By increasing the number of states and complexity of the transition rules from one configuration to another, we can achieve systems capable of solving even very complex problems.

The relation between previous and subsequent states is deepened in one of the fundamental concepts that Cybernetics focuses on—the feedback mechanism. In a feedback loop, there is a circular arrangement of causally connected elements. By imprinting an initial stimulus, each element acts on the next until the last one acts again on the first one, so that the first connection (input) undergoes the effect of the last (output), thereby resulting in the final self-regulation of the system because each time the entire cycle is completed, the initial effect changes (Capra & Luisi, 2014, p. 89). Machines, the operation of which involves feedback loops, were later called cybernetic machines. In feedback, Wiener also detected the mechanism behind homeostasis, the self-regulation that allows living organisms to maintain a state of dynamic equilibrium.

The Turing machine, circular feedback processes, and principle of homeostatic equilibrium are based on conceptualizations that prove enlightening in understanding how social systems, firms, industries, and markets work.

The cybernetic field was also home to Shannon's information theory and the application of cybernetic models to neural and cognitive processes, thanks mainly to Ashby's work. Both authors, starting from different research, delved into the theme of complexity. Shannon links the complexity of a system to the amount of information likely to be transferred or lost in the system itself, whereas the cybernetic variety model developed by Ashby assesses the complexity of a system in relation to the number of possible states, where each state corresponds to a configuration of the relationships between the constituent processors of the system. Starting from this assessment, Ashby enunciated the "Law of Requisite Variety", with which he affirmed that the variety of results can be decreased, as disturbances increase, only with an equal variety of possible answers because "only variety can destroy variety" (Ashby, 2015, p. 207).[15]

A significant step was made with the transition from the Cybernetics of observed systems to the Cybernetics of observing systems

[15] The statement can be expressed differently, arguing that a control system cannot have a variety lower than that of the controlled system. Ashby's Law of Requisite Variety is frequently recalled in studies on complexity (see, among others, Vicari, 2024, p. 134; Luhmann, 1995, p. 25).

(second-order cybernetics), whose main theories were developed by Heinz von Foerster in the context of the Biological Computer Laboratory, which he founded after his participation in the Macy Conferences. It was von Foerster who introduced the concept of "self-organizing systems," which we will discuss in Chap. 4, wherein theories on self-referential systems will be deepened.

In *Cognitive Psychology*, there have been marked advances toward epistemological approaches that involve complexity. The work of Herbert Simon (Nobel Prize for Economics in 1978) led to a total revision of the mechanism of decision-making processes, thereby overcoming the idea of a positive (substantive) rationality to move toward a conception based on procedural (bounded) rationality, which led to questioning all the logic based on the linearity of cognitive processes. Edgar Morin directly addressed the issue of multidimensional thinking, ambivalence of cognitive processes, and uncertainty of knowledge, thereby encouraging the search for a "method of complexity." Jean Piaget, father of genetic epistemology and founder of the Centre International d'Epistemologie Genetique, overturns the concept that systems have simple processes of adaptation to the environment and introduces the idea that systems select stimuli from outside, thereby distinguishing those that are significant from those that are not significant solely with respect to the objective of their conservation and their identity.[16]

In *Chemistry* and *Physics*, important steps were also taken toward the study of complexity. Classical thermodynamics have dealt with systems in equilibrium or close to equilibrium. With the theory of dissipative structures, Ilya Prigogine (Nobel Prize for Chemistry in 1977) has studied systems far from equilibrium, which maintain and increase their order at the expense of greater disorder in the environment.

The reversibility of phenomena was a fundamental postulate of classical science in which it is always possible to reproduce (even artificially in a laboratory) a condition of transition from a certain "past" toward a certain "future" and in which irregularities were considered a loss of energy.

---

[16] Piaget's concept opens the way to the concept of "enacted environment," which will be taken up in Sect. 5.4, Chap. 5.

Prigogine's speculations re-evaluate the constructive role of nonequilibrium in irreversible processes. Prigogine (2007, p. 156) asserts that the most unexpected result comes from the constructive role of nonequilibrium. Away from equilibrium, coherent states and complex structures that could not exist in a reversible world are created. If we define a dynamic system as a transformation in space from one point to another (Fig. 1.6a), according to classical theory, the probability of finding a point in a given area is 1 (if it is on the appropriate trajectory) or 0 (if it is outside the trajectory). A probabilistic theory, such as that of Prigogine, admits that there may be probabilities other than 0 or 1 because the description may not occur in terms of trajectories but in terms of domain (Fig. 1.6b).

Not knowing with the proper precision the initial condition, which affects the future state of the system, it is not possible to identify *a priori* the trajectory (therefore, we are faced with the dependence on the initial conditions that we had already encountered in the theories on chaos). The fact that the system can assume multiple states makes the structure indeterminate and makes it impossible to predict the final configuration. Far from equilibrium, the molecules are interconnected by multiple feedback rings, described by nonlinear equations, which are of a nonlinear degree. The greater the number of possible solutions, the greater the

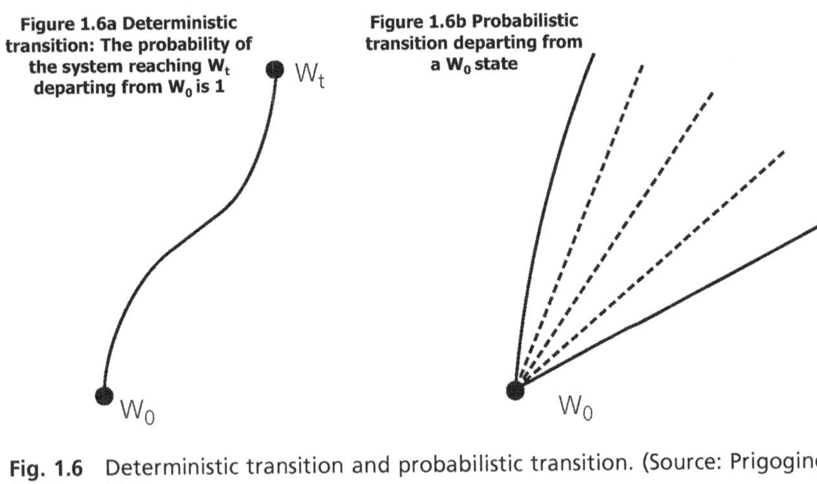

Fig. 1.6 Deterministic transition and probabilistic transition. (Source: Prigogine (2007, p. 164))

distance from equilibrium and the consequent complexity of the system. From this perspective, entropy[17] does not assume the meaning of energy dissipation as in classical thermodynamics but of instability of the dynamic systems.

The role of discontinuities has also been re-evaluated in *Biology* in the context of conceptions on the evolution of species. Charles Darwin, an advocate of the gradualist conception of evolution according to which changes took place imperceptibly with a uniform and continuous rhythm, had already revisited this idea in successive editions of his work, admitting that in evolutionary processes, there could also be variations in rhythm or discontinuity. Stephen J. Gould, with the "theory of punctuated equilibria," radicalized the thesis affirming that in the face of periods in which stability prevails, evolutionary change is often concentrated in instantaneous events of "speciation by bifurcation" (Gould, 2007, pp. 209–210).

The theme of stagnation and discontinuity is central to the analysis of the evolution of the company and fundamental in understanding some rapid upheavals in the configuration of sectors and markets, including sudden changes in the power relations, competitive positions, and cooperative agreements within these entities.

In the biological field, the theories of Francisco Varela and Humberto Maturana on autopoietic systems also developed, which will be included in the in-depth studies on systemic thinking in Chaps. 4–5.

In *Sociology*, great attention is given to complex structures. Luhmann's thinking on social systems, as the cultural background and the conceptual reference base of our interpretative proposal, are presented in Chaps. 4–6, where they will be widely taken up.

The complexity in the relationship between the company and aggregates with which it comes into contact manifests itself through many of the concepts we just presented. The objects of our study are not determined and appear to be not only numerous but also multivalent; their

[17] The most widely used definition of entropy in the economic field is the statistical one by Ludwig Boltzmann. The famous example of the distribution of molecules in a vessel of cold and hot water demonstrates how the most likely state is one in which the molecules mix disorderly with each other rather than arranging themselves neatly (e.g., all cold water molecules on one side and all hot water molecules on the other). From these considerations, it is determined that the transition from order to disorder represents the transition from an unlikely state to a probable state.

relationships are not very stable and, at least apparently, disordered. The possibilities of predicting spatiotemporal connections are scarce because alternative and/or contradictory solutions are equally possible and, in some cases, coexist. Companies, industries, and markets, such as the dissipative structures of Prigogine, often live far from equilibrium. Nevertheless, they increase their energy. For a phenomenon similar to the butterfly effect, small modifications that are generated in a periphery of the systems in consideration can produce enormous consequences in other areas of the systems themselves. The indispensable importance of the starting conditions means that similar, but not coincident, initial entrepreneurial situations produce significant differentiations over time.

References

Arthur, W. B. (2014). *Complexity and the Economy*. Oxford University Press.

Ashby, W. R. (2015). *An Introduction to Cybernetics*. Martino Publishing.

Battiston, S., Farmer, J. D., Flache, A., Garlaschelli, D., Haldane, A. G., Hhesterbeek, H., Hommes, C., Jaeger, C., May, R., & Scheffer, M. (2016). Complexity Theory and Financial Regulation. *Science, 351*(6275), 818–819.

Beinhocker, E. D. (2006). *The Origin of Wealth. Evolution, Complexity, and the Radical Remaking in Economics*. Harvard Business Press.

Beinhocker, E. D. (2013). Reflexivity, Complexity, and the Nature of Social Science. *Journal of Economic Methodology, 20*(4), 330–342.

Boulton, J. G., Allen, P. M., & Bowman, C. (2015). *Embracing Complexity. Strategic Perspective for an Age of Turbulence*. Oxford University Press.

Capra, F. (1997). *The web of life. A new Synthesis of Mind and Matter*. HarperCollins Publishers.

Capra, F., & Luisi, P. (2014). *The Systems View of Life. A Unifying Vision*. Cambridge University Press.

Chamberlin, E. H. (1937). Monopolistic or Imperfect Competition? *The Quarterly Journal of Economics, 51*(4), 557–580.

Coser, L. A. (2012). *Masters of Sociological Thought. Ideas in Historical and Social Context*. Rawat Publications.

Dill, W. R. (1958). Environment as an Influence on Managerial Autonomy. *Administrative Science Quarterly, 2*(4), 409–443.

Dolphin, T., & Nash, D. (Eds.). (2012). *Complex New World. Translating New Economic Thinking into Public Policy*. Institute for Public Policy Research.

Dopfer, K., Foster, J., & Potts, J. (2004). Micro-meso-macro. *Journal of Evolutionary Economics, 14*(2), 263–279.

Durlauf, S. N. (2012). Complexity, Economics, and Public Policy. *Politics, Philosophy & Economics, 11*(1), 45–75.

Fontana, M. (2010). Can Neoclassical Economics Handle Complexity? The fallacy of the Oil Spot Dynamic. *Journal of Economic Behavior & Organization, 76*(3), 584–596.

Foster, J. (2005). From Simplistic to Complex Systems in Economics. *Cambridge Journal of Economics, 29*(4), 873–892.

Gould, S. J. (2007). Il darwinismo e l'ampliamento della teoria evoluzionista. In G. Bocchi & M. Ceruti (Eds.). *La sfida della complessità*. Bruno Mondadori Editori.

Grimm, V., Revilla, E., Berger, U., Jeltsch, F., Mooij, W. M., Railsback, S. F., Thulke, H., Weiner, J., Wiegand, T., & Deangelis, D. (2005). Pattern-Oriented Modeling of Agent-Based Complex Systems: Lessons from Ecology. *Science, 310*(5750), 987–991.

Heise, A. (2017). Whither Economic Complexity? A new heterodox Economic Paradigm or Just Another Variation within the Mainstream? *International Journal of Pluralism and Economics Education, 8*(2), 115–129.

Helbing, D., & Kirman, A. (2013). Rethinking Economics Using Complexity Theory. *Real-World Economics Review. 64*. Retrieved July 10, 2023, from https://papers.ssrn.com/sol3/papers.cfm?abstract_id=2292370

Hill, S. A., & Gergoulas, S. (2016). Internal Corporate Venturing: A Review of (almost) Five Decades of Literature. In S. A. Zahra, J. Hayton, & D. O. Neubaum (Eds.), *Handbook of Corporate Entrepreneurship*. Edward Elgar.

Holt, R. P. F., Rosser, J. J. B., & Colander, D. (2011). The Complexity Era in Economics. *Review of Political Economy, 23*(3), 357–369.

Kirman, A. (2004). Economics and Complexity. *Advances in Complex Systems, 7*(2), 139–155.

Kirman, A. (2016). Complexity and Economic Policy: A Paradigm Shift or a Change in Perspective? A Review Essay on David Colander and Roland Kupers's Complexity and the Art of Public Policy. *Journal of Economic Literature, 54*(2), 534–572.

Landreth, H., & Colander, D. C. (1994). *History of Economic Thought*. Houghton Mifflin.

Le Moigne, J. (2007). Progettazione della complessità e complessità della progettazione. In G. Bocchi & M. Ceruti (Eds.). *La sfida della complessità*. Bruno Mondadori Editori.

Lorenz, E. N. (1972). *Predictability; Does the Flap of a Butterfly's Wings in Brazil Set Off a Tornado in Texas?* Paper Presented at the 139th Meeting of The American Association for the Advancement of Science. Massachusetts Institute of Technology, Mass. USA, 29 December 1972.

Luhmann, N. (1995). *Social Systems*. Standford University Press.

Luhmann, N. (2016). *Gesellschaftsstruktur und Semantik. Studien zur Wissenssoziologie der modernen Gesellschaft. Band 2*. Suhrkamp.

Mann, S. (Ed.). (2011). *Sectors Matter!: Exploring Mesoeconomics*. Springer-Verlag.

Miller, H. M., & Page, S. E. (2007). *Complex Adaptive Systems. An Introduction to Computational Models of Social Life*. Princeton University Press.

Mitleton-Kelly, E. (Ed.). (2003). *Complex systems and Evolutionary Perspectives on Organisations: The Application of Complexity Theory to Organisations*. Elsevier Science.

Morin, E. (2007). Le vie della complessità. In G. Bocchi & M. Ceruti (Eds.), *La sfida della complessità*. Bruno Mondadori Editori.

Newell, A., & Simon, H. E. (1972). *Human Problem Solving*. Prentice Hall.

Parisi, G., & Ceruti, M. (2013). *Cosa significa complessità*. Retrieved October 11, 2021, from https://www.complexityinstitute.it/

Peitgen, H., & Richter, P. H. (1986). *The beauty of Fractals: Images of Complex Dynamical Systems*. Springer-Verlag.

Pheby, J. (1990). *Methodology and Economics. A Critical Introduction*. The Macmillan Press.

Prigogine, I. (2007). L'esplorazione della complessità. In M. Ceruti & Bocchi G. (Eds) *La sfida della complessità*. Bruno Mondadori Editori.

Rullani, E. (2004). *La fabbrica dell'immateriale. Produrre valore con la conoscenza*. Carocci.

Salzano, M., & Colander, D. (Eds.). (2007). *Complexity Hints for Economic Policy*. Springer-Verlag.

Tain, D. (2021). Capitalizing on Complexity in Modern Businesses Environments: A Network-Based Perspective for Projects and Organizations. *The Journal of Applied Business and Economics, 23*(1), 29–41.

Vicari, S. (2024). *The Living Firm. Journey into a Different Conception*. Amazon Publishing.

Vicari, S., & Bertoli, G. (2000). Diversificazione, acquisizioni, apprendimento. In S. Podestà & F. Golfetto (Eds.), *La nuova concorrenza. Contesti di interazione, strumenti di azione, approcci di analisi*. Egea.

2

Firms, Industries, Markets: The Unavoidable Issues for Scientific Research

Abstract The terms firm, industry, and market are not associable with uniquely determinable entities. The complexity in Economics and, in particular, in micro, meso, and macro relationships is caused by the presence of multiple forms of the studied objects, by the indeterminacy of results, by the instability of structures, and, at the same time, by the birth of epistemological standards that invite the use of new perspectives to read the company world and the aggregates close to it.

In relation to the topic of micro, meso, and macro relationships in the *Economics of Complexity*, we focus on four themes of scientific research, which are connected to each other, yet with autonomous insights concerning both content and methodology:

- The complexity and consequent opacity of the entities being studied, that is, of the company and the meso and macroaggregates with which it relates (industries and markets, above all).
- The difficulty of identifying boundaries between these entities.
- The unpredictability of the results of the micro, meso, and macro relationships.
- The plurality of possible views on micro, meso, and macro relationships and the scientific judgment on these relationships.

C. Mazzoni, *Firms, Industries, Markets*, https://doi.org/10.1007/978-3-031-59823-4_2

Keywords The topics of scientific research • The complexity of the objects of study • The difficulty in establishing boundaries • The unpredictability of relationship outcomes • The plurality of possible views on micro, meso and macro relationships and the scientific judgment on them • Militant positivism • Élitist authoritianism • Epistemological anarchism • Constructivism

2.1 The Topics of Scientific Research

The terms firm, industry, and market are not associable with uniquely determinable entities. As previously stated, the complexity in Economics and, in particular, in micro, meso, and macro relationships is caused by the presence of multiple forms of the studied objects, by the indeterminacy of results, by the instability of structures, and, at the same time, by the birth of epistemological standards that invite the use of new perspectives to read the company world and the aggregates close to it.

In relation to the topic discussed herein, with respect to the numerous questions raised by the *Economics of Complexity*, we can focus on four themes of scientific research, which are connected to each other, yet with autonomous insights concerning both content and methodology:

- The complexity and consequent opacity of the entities being studied, that is, of the company and the meso and macroaggregates with which it relates (industries and markets, above all).
- The difficulty of identifying boundaries between these entities.
- The unpredictability of the results of the micro, meso, and macro relationships.
- The plurality of possible views on micro, meso, and macro relationships and the scientific judgment on these relationships.

2.2 The Complexity of the Objects of Study

Currently, the first problematic element regarding the in-depth analysis of micro, meso, and macro relationships is the complexity and the consequent opacity of the objects of our study. At first glance, we could say that this is the root of the matter, the primary aspect from which others derive.

A defining discomfort and a difficulty in relating to precisely identified objects are noted because of the number of contributions that raise, from various perspectives, the problems of identifying the "company" element, on the one hand, and its meso and macro elements of reference, on the other.

In this sense, it is no coincidence that the attempt to define the company and the meso and macroaggregates of reference makes increasing use of metaphors. The metaphor can be an important tool of knowledge, particularly when new conceptualizations and paradigms emerge.

One of the metaphors that can be used to represent the company in the *Economics of Complexity* is that of the hologram.[1] In a hologram, each portion contains all the information of the whole in which it participates, so each individual element can be useful to reconstruct the entire system, even if each part maintains its own individuality (Morin, 2007, p. 28). Karl Pribram used the holographic metaphor for the representation of the brain: holograms, in fact, distribute information throughout the coding structure so that all information is contained in each single part and the entire image can be built from each single part (Pribram, 2007, p. 239). This abstraction can facilitate the understanding of the company as a complex system, consisting of elements that are part of the entirety but that, in turn, contain the whole, at least to some extent.

The holographic metaphor is also applicable to meso- and macroaggregates of reference. Here too, complex structures coexist that integrate and oppose each other at the same time, and in which unity is found by reconstructing the parts, yet also within the parts themselves. In truth, the defining discomfort referred to in relation to the objects of our study finds its highest expression precisely in the specification of the sector and markets and on the positioning of the company within them. There are numerous views on the phenomenon, attributable to different logics and paradigms, as will be more widely analyzed in Chap. 3. The

[1] The hologram reproduces a three-dimensional image on a two-dimensional support (film or plate). Each part of the media contains all the information; thus, if we cut the hologram into numerous parts, each part will show the image in its entirety.

plurality of approaches has also multiplied the proposals for interpretation and attempts to classify existing models.

The attempt to schematize the various possible approaches and the frequent use of alternative terms to identify the task environment (e.g., competitive arena, strategic business area) imply the need to seek a reading that can interpret (rather than mitigate) the complexity of the identified objects of study.

It should be stressed that this interpretation also has a self-reflective value. As previously mentioned, the company (but the same can be said for other operators performing in the industry and in the various markets) also acts—within the micro, meso, and macro context—as an observing subject. In this sense, the firm is interested in knowing the environment it refers to, but it also needs to understand itself and its boundaries (in some way, it must define or interpret itself). As a result, the complexity of the micro, meso, and macro relationships is continuously fed by the complexity of the objects but also by that of the participating subjects.

2.3 The Difficulty in Establishing Boundaries

In a simplified reading of micro, meso, and macro relationships, as shown in Fig. 1.2, the boundaries between the company, the industry, and the markets are defined and stable. In an analysis based on complexity, boundaries are perceived but are not precisely determined. In Fig. 1.3, the boundaries between the different systems identified (perimeters of the rectangles) are dashed to indicate their permeability and instability. In many cases, they also overlap and intertwine. Where is the boundary of a company within a network? Is it the entire network or is it the boundary of the individual company participating in it? The entities under study are delimited from an observation perspective rather than in an objective manner.

The definition of boundaries is made more difficult by their spatiotemporal instability. As can be implied at this point of the analysis, in fact, it should be noted that the objects of the study are not only complex but also constantly changing and between micro units and meso- and macroeconomic aggregates, there is a continuous potential dynamism. Actors who initially form part of an agglomeration, over time, may move elsewhere (the arrows in Fig. 1.3 represent this): through a vertical integration downstream, suppliers can become competitors, as well as distributors, who integrate upstream or produce private labels; the human resources that promote competitive spin-off projects are initially part of the company but later become competitors and, therefore, elements of the reference macrocontext. Powerful factors of innovation, both technological and functional, lead the company toward processes of decentralization or, *vice versa*, of integration; of boundary extension or, on the contrary, narrowing. The examples could multiply, especially in the presence of companies increasingly dematerialized in terms of architectures and production processes.

A scarce recognition of boundaries also undermines the dimensional conceptions of the objects of study: it is not easy to define the extension of a commercial company placed in a distribution chain without resorting to a series of specifications, just as it is impossible to measure the magnitude of meso and macroaggregates in the presence of converging processes (which lead to the approximation of industries and markets that were originally different) or diverging processes (in the presence of diversifications driven by specialization and the search for niches). Sector or market definitions that are too broad could jeopardize the possibility of studying interconnections, whereas definitions that are too narrow could lead to disregarding elements of interest for the analysis.

By losing the possibility of defining the dimension, the possibility of quantitatively measuring the phenomena is also lost: how big is the position of a small company in an industrial condominium? How measurable is the extent of a company in a district or in a network? As the mathematics of complexity teaches us,[2] it will likely be necessary to move from numerical and quantitative computation methods to qualitative measurements.

2.4 The Unpredictability of Relationship Outcomes

As we have seen, one of the recurring elements in the epistemology of complexity is the impossibility of making forecasts and, as a result, the inability to know in advance the trajectories and the results of the micro,

---

[2] See Sect. 1.4.1, Chap. 1.

meso, and macro interaction. The generation and distribution of value, when considered as a result of the micro, meso, and macro interaction, is spread across overlapping portions of space and discontinuous units of time. The difficulty of making predictions (but also the difficulty of studying relationships while they occur) also derives from the interdependence of behaviors: as in the Boolean networks described in Sect. 1.4.1, Chap. 1, at time $t + 1$, the system's configuration depends not only on the operators' status at time t but also on their reciprocal position.

The amount of information to be kept under control to be able to make decisions in complex conditions should reconstruct not only all data on the initial situation of observation but also any possible interdependence between the factors under investigation, which is obviously not feasible. To improve the forecast reliability, the survey tools that help the entrepreneurial interpretations of the micro, meso, and macro relationships have multiplied, especially relying on the digital transformation and using Artificial Intelligence: consumer profiling and purchasing behavior, analysis of the motivation of human resources, studies on financial markets, and modeling of distribution circuits are all attempts to enhance the knowledge of current reality to anticipate the possible consequences of future choices.

In addition to the complexity and interdependence of behaviors and the cumulative effects deriving from them, the inability to predict the relationship results is also caused by the need to study the phenomena at the same time as the elements determining them are moving. As we already mentioned, in this context, the company, in its capacity as a decision-maker, is in a dual condition: on the one hand, it is one of the objects of the relation and, on the other hand, it has to interpret and, as far as possible, predict the results of the relationship consequent to its behavior. For example, a company wishing to evaluate the launch of a new product in advance will be forced to move in relation to its current position: it will conduct research on potential buyers in test markets; it will notify suppliers and distributors; and it will require the intervention of investors to support the project. The very fact of having carried out these actions will influence the behavior of the other actors involved: consumers will start to form expectations about the new product;

competitors will evaluate the implementation of reactive maneuvers; suppliers and distributors will move along the supply chains and, probably, all these movements will generate disorderly and unexpected effects, which will in turn influence the system of interdependent reactions and will change the configuration of the overall micro, meso, and macro system, even before or at the same time as the launch of the new product. Therefore, being the company itself an object of the relationship as well as an observer (and, moreover, a complex, noncompact, and often polycellular observer and, therefore, with internal views that do not always coincide), it is forced to produce the observation (and the related forecast) at the same time as it operates. In the example, it must foresee the consequences of the launch of the new product while acting to manage the activities related to the launch itself. We have seen in Sect. 1.4.1, Chap. 1, how, in Physics, Heisenberg's uncertainty principle demonstrates that the observation of the phenomenon itself compromises its result; in the case of companies, the self-observation to which they submit when acting in their reference environment (and the related representation that they give) ends up influencing to some extent the result of the relationship, making it impossible to put in a sequence the observation, the action, and the result achieved, without influencing the linearity of the sequence.

An in-depth study of the difficulties of predicting the results of the micro, meso and macro relationship can be carried out using the "non-trivial machine" concept, where the term machine refers generically to the functional properties of an abstract entity and not necessarily to something consisting of gears, buttons and levers (von Foerster, 2003). The components of the relationship (the company and the task environment) as well as the relationship itself are non-trivial machines in which the input–output correspondence is not predetermined.[3] In recursive circularity, the result is also influenced by the output previously provided. This determines the unpredictability of the resulting events because the output is destined to be modified in subsequent experiments, even with the same initial inputs.

---

[3] On this topic, see also Vicari (2024, pp. 8–9).

2.5 The Plurality of Possible Views on Micro, Meso, and Macro Relationships and the Scientific Judgment on Them

The relativity of categories according to the perspectives of observation of a third subject (or even the perspective of self-observation of one of the elements of the relationship, e.g., the company) brings to the center of the debate the question of subjectivity and the multiplicity of points of view in the interpretation of the observed systems by the observing system. The diversity of possible representations suggests alternative views of reality: the Epistemology and the Philosophy of Science have been wondering for centuries whether some of these views (theories) can be considered more reliable than others and on what methodological parameters a theory/view should be based on to be defined as "scientific." Accordingly, in the presence of theories that present different interpretations with respect to a given problem, the question arises whether some of them are better than others and, in general, what are the criteria to judge a theory as reliable from a scientific point of view.

As we have seen, one of the most delicate conceptual steps of the movement of complexity, with respect to the dogmas of classical science, is the emergence of an epistemology of complexity that provides for the simultaneous presence of multiple views/theories and, above all, contemplates the inclusion of the observer in the process of generating knowledge.

Going back to the subject matter of our discussion, there are different interpretations about the micro, meso, and macro relationships that are based on different cognitive objectives and logical assumptions.[4]

The marginalist microeconomics, for example, interprets micro, meso, and macro relationships starting from a hypothesis of perfect competition and perfectly rational actions by the actors involved in the process, which allows the macro to originate from the simple sum of microeconomic initiatives (the total consumers demand is obtained from the sum of the individual demand curves based on the utility functions of

---

[4] The topic will be discussed in Chap. 3.

individual consumers, and the total supply curve is determined by the sum of the choices made by producers within their production function). The hypotheses underlying the interpretative model make it possible to predict a series of chain consequences on production factors, on the substitutability of goods, on the determination of the equilibrium price, etc.

The structuralist model of Industrial Organization, on the other hand, provides that micro behaviors descend from the constraints imposed by the presence of the company within a sector (mesoeconomic space), with predefined conditions in terms of barriers, concentration of demand and supply, possibility of price maneuvers, etc.

The approach of strategic management schools presents an even different view: assuming the existence of an external environment that is difficult to decipher in its entirety, it is the company that defines the strategic maneuvers to be carried out to obtain the maximum competitive advantage compared to competitors by carefully studying consumers, competitors, strengths, and weaknesses of its organization and consequently planning its action on the market.

These different logics of interpretation of the relationship between the company and the meso and macrocontexts of reference were then reinterpreted and revisited. In some cases, they moved away from the initial approach, while in others, they saved the original conceptual corpus. Which of these views should we consider as being the right one? Can they all be judged as equally valid, perhaps admitting that they derive from different cultural backgrounds and that, therefore, they are also influenced by the intellectual background, observation conditions, and cognitive objectives of the scholars who have proposed them? In relation to the observed system, then, what is the relevance of the position of the observing subject, and how much can the latter be judged to be impartial, objective in his/her exploration?

As already mentioned, Epistemology has always tried to identify the criteria by which one theory can be considered better than another and to separate science from what is not scientific. This is one of the oldest topics in the Philosophy of Science, on which there has always been an open debate with different criteria prevailing at different times. In this regard, we thought it interesting to briefly summarize which schools of thought influence contemporary epistemological thinking on the subject in question.[5]

2.5.1 Militant Positivism

For militant positivists (this is how the current heirs of classical positivism are defined by Lakatos), the theme of the demarcation between science and nonscience takes on, with different degrees, a connotation similar to that of traditional culture. Positivists believe that there is an objective possibility (or, in any case, an accredited method) to verify the validity of a theory and therefore to affirm whether it has a scientific character or not. According to Lakatos, the representatives of militant positivism can be grouped into a movement comprising various schools: *classical inductivism*, *conventionalism*, and *falsificationism* (Lakatos & Feyerabend, 1999, p. 33).

According to *classical inductivism*, it is necessary to deduce theories from facts. However, in the twentieth century, less extreme versions have also been proposed which, in admitting the difficulty of deducing theories from facts, believe that the latter can at least make theoretical deductions probable (*probabilism*) or believe that only assertions whose value is decidable through an experiment (*verificationism*) have meaning.

In Economics, and in Management in particular, this logic is used by all the studies that subject hypotheses to verification on the basis of experimental analyses, mainly carried out on the basis of statistical–mathematical methodologies,[6] defining the acceptability or otherwise of the initial hypotheses on the basis of the results (and their statistical significance).

---

[5] The discussion on the currents of thought is present, except for the section on constructivism, in some lectures on the method given by Imre Lakatos in 1973 at the Department of Philosophy, Logic and Scientific Method, London School of Economics (reported in Lakatos & Feyerabend, 1999).

[6] In this effort to expand and manage information, the methodological heritage of experimental sciences was, in fact, extended to Management (but generally to all Social Sciences), for example, using sample statistics.

According to *conventionalism*, theories *per se* are not true or false. Rather, they are conventions, tools that help formulate predictions. This current is also called instrumentalism, and in some ways, economist Milton Friedman's position is included in it (Pheby, 1990, pp. 81–94). In Economics, the instrumentalist approach accepts theories that make it possible to make forecasts, for example, in terms of Economic Policy. In Management, this formation is often implicit in some positions that attribute great value to regulatory aspects, capable of suggesting to managers or entrepreneurs the most suitable behavior for a certain situation.

Finally, according to *falsificationism*, which finds its main advocate in Popper (1959, 1972, 1983), there are some preconditions allowing us to endorse the best hypotheses, namely, those that are closest to reality: when faced with a scientific problem, it is first necessary to propose a coherent hypothesis—that is, one relating to the underlying problem—and that, possibly, can be empirically verifiable. Second, it is necessary to specify under which conditions the theory can be falsified. The active and continuous use of falsification to eliminate dubious hypotheses ensures scientific progress. If the theory is falsified, a new theory must be formulated that satisfies the same conditions but does not progress based on exceptions:

> To give a very simple-minded example: suppose you put forward that all swans are white, and then produce a black swan. You have to reject "All swans are white." Let us call the black swan "Peter." According to Popper you are not allowed to put forward the new theory "All swans are white, except for Peter," because this is an ad hoc manoeuvre, and this kind of exception-barring is not allowed...just remember this Newtonian business: after all, we had a hundred anomalies in 1686. And what the scientists actually did was to shelve these anomalies and say: "The Newtonian theory is all right except for these hundred or so anomalies." (Lakatos & Feyerabend, 1999, pp. 84–85)

At a given moment in history, the dominant theory will be that which explains a wide range of empirical observations and which has not yet been falsified (Landreth & Colander, 1994, p. 12). Therefore, the Popperian approach is based on the realism of the hypotheses and on seeking experimental confirmation. However, unlike the more classic approach of positivism, he admits that there is no possibility of proving a certain theory but only of rejecting it. Until a theory is falsified, albeit actively trying to do so, it will be strengthened and will indirectly take on greater credibility.

Although Popperian positions are often considered at the frontier of modern epistemology, they are, as said, fundamentally based on realism, on the belief that "there is an objective reality to the word waiting to be discovered" (Pheby, 1990, p. 26).

2.5.2 Élitist Authoritianism

This current of thought, mainly represented by Kuhn (1962), believes that the demarcation between science and nonscience is based on the judgment of the scientific community of reference. Kuhn argues that there is a dominant paradigm in scientific communities (which derives from the adoption of a particular view of the world): to be considered as such, the paradigm must attract a stable number of adherents and, moreover, it must leave open a certain number of questions, which will constitute a subject of research by new affiliates in periods of "normal science." The presence of anomalies in itself is not sufficient to lead to the dismissal of the paradigm. For this to happen, there must be the proposal of a new paradigm explaining the anomalies better than the previous one: every time an old paradigm is replaced by a new one, we are in the presence of a "scientific revolution."

The Kuhnian conception lends itself to absorbing the potential coming from different conceptions of reality. When Kuhn affirms that the modification of the paradigm does not involve a change of the world but rather of our view of it (Pheby, 1990, p. 41), he somehow admits the decline of knowledge based on the effort to reveal objective realities to come to a conception of knowledge in which the observer becomes part of the game through the perceptual parameters and the interpretative codes available. We can, then, agree or disagree that the academic community should decide what the right paradigm is and that it has all the information to make this choice.[7]

---

[7] On this subject, see Lakatos and Feyerabend (1999, pp. 28–31).

2.5.3 Epistemological Anarchism

This approach, which in some ways takes up the canons of *scepticism* or *cultural relativism*, has been interpreted in more recent times by Paul Feyerabend, author of the famous text *Against method. Outline of an anarchistic theory of knowledge* (1975). According to this epistemological view, there is no truth, and every scientific theory is a set of beliefs, like many others. When one theory overcomes another,[8] it becomes the truth (according to this approach, the truth is the opinion of the winner). Therefore, there is no progress but rather a change in the system of opinions:

> There is no view, however, "absurd" or "immoral," he (the epistemological anarchist) refuses to consider or to act upon, and no method he regards as indispensable. The only thing he opposes positively and absolutely are universal standards, universal laws, universal ideas such as "Truth," "Justice," "Honesty," "Reason" and the behavior they engender, though he does not deny that it is often good policy to act as if such laws (such standards, such ideas) existed and as if he believed in them. (Lakatos & Feyerabend, 1999, p. 115)

2.5.4 Constructivism

According to this approach, reality is a construction of those who observe and study it. Therefore, the knowledge process is also the result of the cognitive structures of the subject who proposes to represent it and the contingent context in which the analysis takes place. In this sense, the observer takes on an active role in the knowledge process. The constructivist approach is probably the most congenial one to the epistemology of complexity, where the existence of an objective scientific description and a privileged method of observation are questioned, while a plurality of

[8] In a logic in which there is no scientific truth to prove, the victory of one theory over another occurs because it is better constructed or argued. "The *rhetorical approach* to methodology emphasizes the persuasiveness of language, contending that a theory may be accepted not because it is inherently true but because its advocates succeed in convincing others of its value by means of their superior rhetoric" (Landreth & Colander, 1994, p. 14).

points of view and methodologies seem to coexist, which contribute to making the process of knowledge even more complex. It is no coincidence that scholars who are particularly close to complex thought are included among the main exponents of this epistemological current—scholars such as Edgar Morin, Jean Piaget, Niklas Luhmann, Humberto Maturana, Francisco Varela, and Heinz von Foerster, who are often cited in this volume.[9]

In constructivism, observers enter the process of knowledge, bringing forth their view of the world.[10] Observers are in the society they observe and yet, at the same time, according to the holographic metaphor, society is in them, they are possessed by the culture they possess (Morin, 2007, p. 30). In this sense, it was said that all the different theoretical perspectives of observation of micro, meso, and macro relations are affected by the observations made by the scholars who proposed them, and the cultural substratum of those who propose a certain view of the world influences the proposal itself. The question of the position of the observer in the analysis of a phenomenon, of the influence of his/her methodological and epistemological approach, of the possible coexistence of different—often equally accredited—views is intertwined with the issues of self-observation and the point of view of the company itself (and of the other systems that act within the relationship) as an observant subject.

In Chap. 4, therefore, we will try to approach a theoretical perspective compatible with the uncertainty that characterizes the relationship and its elements and, at the same time, that takes into account the multiplicity of possible views. In Chap. 5, the four issues of the research on micro, meso, and macro relationships, presented here as the key point in question, will be reviewed considering an interpretative proposal. This proposal, far from wanting to represent a definitive answer to the questions posed, can represent a possible perspective of analysis, one of the many views admissible in the study of the micro, meso, and macro relationship in the *Economics of Complexity*.

---

[9] For an interesting series of contributions on constructivism, see Watzlawick (1984).

[10] In this sense, the properties of the organization are also a function of the observer, particularly of the specific relationship generated between the observer and the object being observed (Vicari, 2024, p. 24).

References

Feyerabend, P. K. (1975). *Against Method: Outline of an Anarchistic Theory of Knowledge*. New Left Books.

Kuhn, T. S. (1962). *The Structure of Scientific Revolutions. The University of Chicago Press*. Illinois.

Lakatos, I., & Feyerabend, P. (1999). *For and Against Method*. The University Chicago Press.

Landreth, H., & Colander, D. C. (1994). *History of Economic Thought*. Houghton Mifflin.

Morin, E. (2007). Le vie della complessità. In G. Bocchi & M. Ceruti (Eds.), *La sfida della complessità*. Bruno Mondadori Editori.

Pheby, J. (1990). *Methodology and Economics. A Critical Introduction*. The Macmillan Press.

Popper, K. (1959). *The Logic of Scientific Discovery*. Hutchinson.

Popper, K. (1972). *Conjectures and Refutations*. Routledge and Kegan Paul.

Popper, K. (1983). In W. W. Bartley III (Ed.), *Realism and the Aim of Science. Volume I From the Postscript to the Logic of Scientific Discovery*. Hutchinson.

Pribram, K. (2007). Contributi sulla complessità: le scienze neurologiche e le scienze del comportamento. In G. Bocchi & M. Ceruti (Eds.), *La sfida della complessità*. Bruno Mondadori Editori.

Vicari, S. (2024). *The Living Firm. Journey into a Different Conception*. Amazon Publishing.

von Foerster, H. (2003). Perception of the Future and the Future of Perception. In H. von Foerster (Ed.), *Understanding Understanding. Essays on Cybernetics and Cognition*. Springer Verlag.

Watzlawick, P. (Ed.). (1984). *The Invented Reality. How Do We Know What We Believe We Know? Contributions to Constructivism*. W. W. Norton & Company.

3

The Micro, Meso, and Macro Relationships in Economic Thought and "Turning Points"

Abstract In this chapter we try to identify the various "theoretical perspectives" to which the analysis of the micro, meso, and macro relationships in economic theory may be attributed. The term "theoretical perspective" in this context refers not to a single theory but to a vision underlying several theories sharing the same mode of the general interpretation of phenomena. In this sense, it is more general than a theory or a model; it is a structure of thought and a generator of theories or models.

We propose to summarize the different theoretical perspectives of the micro, meso, and macro relationships in four basic conceptualizations:

- The *mechanical–aggregative* theoretical perspective
- The *causal–structuralist* theoretical perspective
- The *strategic–competitive* theoretical perspective
- The *complex systems'* theoretical perspective.

In addition to identifying each approach, this reconstruction includes an additional hypothesis: it is held that the first three schemes for explaining the micro, meso, and macro relationships, consolidated in different ways in the tradition of economic thought, experienced "turning points" that

C. Mazzoni, *Firms, Industries, Markets*, https://doi.org/10.1007/978-3-031-59823-4_3

forced the initial paradigm to take on board some elements of complexity emerging in the real world. The shifts in the paradigm share the cultural orientation of the original structure and revisit some elements but still without aiming to overturn the starting framework. Often, however, without necessarily seeking to do so, such turning points demolished a significant part of the original assumptions.

Keywords The various theoretical perspectives to interpret micro, meso, and macro relationships • The mechanical aggregative theoretical perspective • Turning points in the mechanical aggregative theoretical perspective • The causal structuralist theoretical perspective • Turning points in the causal structuralist theoretical perspective • The strategic competitive theoretical perspective • Turning points in the strategic competitive theoretical perspective • The characteristics of decision-making processes in the various theoretical perspectives • Toward the complex systems' theoretical perspective

3.1 The Various Theoretical Perspectives to Interpret Micro, Meso, and Macro Relationships

Before delving into the interpretative proposal of the following chapters of this work, we first try to identify the various theoretical perspectives to which the analysis of the micro, meso, and macro relationships in economic theory may be attributed: their differences but also their contiguities and their evolution. As previously mentioned, the meaning of the term "theoretical perspective" in this context refers not to a single theory but to a vision underlying several theories sharing the same mode of the general interpretation of phenomena. In this sense, a theoretical perspective is more general than a theory or a model. It is a structure of thought and a generator of theories or models.

The contextualization of the strands of thought in theoretical perspectives and the identification of that which we will define as "turning points toward complexity" are, of course, affected by a personal reinterpretation of the thought of numerous authors, even very distant from one another. Therefore, there is no claim to provide a general taxonomy but rather a subjective interpretation specifically addressed to the subject in question.

We propose to summarize the different theoretical perspectives of the micro, meso, and macro relationships in four basic conceptualizations:

- The *mechanical–aggregative* theoretical perspective
- The *causal–structuralist* theoretical perspective
- The *strategic–competitive* theoretical perspective
- The *complex systems'* theoretical perspective (which provides the interpretative context of the proposal outlined in the following chapters).

In addition to identifying each approach, this reconstruction of the theoretical analysis of the micro, meso, and macro relationships includes an additional hypothesis: it is held that the first three schemes for explaining the micro, meso, and macro relationships, consolidated in different ways in the tradition of economic thought, experienced "turning points" that forced the initial paradigm to take on board some elements of complexity emerging in the real world. Some authors, very often from within the original orthodoxy or following advances in knowledge in related fields, attempted to prop up the initial theoretical structure while inevitably undermining a few basic aspects. In other words, the shifts in the paradigm share the cultural orientation of the original structure and revisit some elements but still without aiming to overturn the starting framework. Often, however, without necessarily seeking to do so, such turning points demolished a significant part of the original assumptions.

The identification of specific turning points stems from an expository need. In reality, they are the product of a gradual process that derives from the incessant debate within each doctrine, in some cases stimulated by impulses from intellectual movements occurring in contiguous areas of scientific thought. Therefore, the concept of "turning point" used in this volume highlights the internal modification of a certain theoretical corpus, which, while saving a large portion of the traditional vision, captures the evolutionary germs implicit in every cognitive interpretation and imprints slightly divergent movements concerning the original structure. Therefore, turning points do not show a scientific revolution à la

Kuhn, with the replacement of one paradigm with another, but rather moments of internal reformism dictated by a continuist perspective of the initial logic.

We will hereafter briefly mention the conceptualizations that, according to the interpretation proposed, refer to the aforementioned first three theoretical perspectives and the relative turning points toward complexity.

3.2 The Mechanical–Aggregative Theoretical Perspective

The original—and in many ways orthodox—formulation of the mechanical–aggregative approach lies in the theoretical framework provided by marginalist microeconomics. Below, we briefly outline its theoretical underpinnings to clarify the use of the method for characterizing this particular expository scheme for the relationship between firms and markets. The neoclassical school[1] took the key step of going beyond the theory of value of the classical school. For the authors of the classical school, the value of a good was determined by the cost of factors of production used to create it. All three founders of the neoclassical school (Jevons, Menger, and Walras) came in parallel to the idea that the value of a good was rather ascribed to the utility of owning such goods. As is well known, this approach analyzes price formation mechanisms and exploits the concept of marginal utility and especially the law of decreasing marginal utility. According to the latter, the utility of the last unit consumed decreases with the increase in the quantity of the good itself owned overall. Hence, consumers maximize overall utility, leveling the marginal utility of all goods owned, that is, pushing each purchase to the point where the utilities of the last units are the same. Among the first-generation authors, Walras sought a general equilibrium model of the market in which mathematical relationships were used to link consumer utility functions with their demand curves. Walras' formulation of general market equilibrium

[1] We refer to the strand of economic theory that developed in the period 1870–1930, referring to the work of three founding fathers (William Stanley Jevons, Carl Menger, and Leon Walras) and the subsequent inquiries by Friedrich von Wieser, Eugen Böhm von Bawerk, Alfred Marshall, and Vilfredo Pareto.

(in which the formation of prices in all markets is studied simultaneously) and the subsequent wording of the partial equilibrium model (i.e., of an individual market) by Marshall are illuminating for the subject at hand.

Given that all goods are homogeneous within the same market, the demand curve is, for most goods, a decreasing function of price. This allows us to sum the individual demand curves of each consumer and plot the total market demand curve, which is likely to also be a decreasing function of price.

With a similar mechanism, producers minimize production costs, choosing the combination between the quantities of factors of production to use in the production function (e.g., the optimal combination of capital and labor). Studying the characteristics of the producer's costs, marginalist economics draws the individual supply curves as increasing functions of the price at which the product can be sold. Since the assumption of the analysis is that of a perfectly competitive market in which all the goods are homogeneous and the only variable is price, in this case, it will also be possible to sum the individual supply curves, thus arriving at the general market supply curve.

Combining consumer equilibrium theory with producer equilibrium theory, we arrive at the definition of market equilibrium, in which the analytical assumptions (agent rationality, perfectly competitive markets, access to complete information on the part of producers and consumers, and free entry to, and exit from, markets) ensure automatic achievement of equilibrium at the intersection of market demand and supply. At this point, the equilibrium price is also defined.

Based on the brief notes listed above, it is, therefore, possible to account for the term used to characterize this *mechanical–aggregative* theoretical perspective. Macroeconomic equilibrium is produced thanks to the sum (*aggregation*) of the behavior of microeconomic agents—consumers and producers—who automatically (*mechanically*) perform predeterminable operations thanks to great simplifications, which are posed as prerequisites of choice processes: full subjective rationality and the consequent search for optimal solutions, perfectly competitive markets (also of factors of production) with relative freedom of entry/exit to/from the market and the parallel condition of price-takers of firms, complete information for all actors, absence of behavioral interdependence, and *a priori* definition of the structure variables (technology, consumer taste, institutional framework). In this context, firms are very simplified entities that operate according to pre-established rules and in a uniform context. Markets are institutions able to process exchanges and are reconstructed through an algorithm that sums microbehaviors linearly.

Despite the simplifications underpinning the analysis, neoclassical economics is one of the few theoretical approaches that weld with precision the microeconomic (theory of the consumer and producer) with the macroeconomic level (market equilibrium): to achieve this link, it must inevitably resort to a high level of abstraction, simplifying the hypotheses underpinning the model. It should also be noted that this expository scheme for the micro, meso, and macro relationships stems from both its historical dimension and its cognitive intent. Indeed, marginalist theory became established at a time when firms and markets did not have the same complexity as that in the present-day context. Simultaneously, its aim was not so much to explain the specific nature of firms and their strategic potential as to provide a general model to illustrate the price formation mechanism.

3.2.1 Turning Points in the Mechanical–Aggregative Theoretical Perspective

Over time, the construction of the marginalist microeconomics has been overcome by visions, which, while anchored to a rationalist subjectivism, have taken note of a general shift, in the phenomenical reality, toward a greater complexity of intersubjective relationships and lower automatic determination of optimizing behavior.

In particular, three deviations toward complexity have been identified, which can be considered important examples of turning points. These are unlikely to be the only ones and, as a result, should be considered examples. The choice of these turning points, among the many possible ones, was made concerning two factors: the importance they had within the paradigm and in the subsequent scientific debate and the potential for contamination of the original apparatus without implying a definitive overcoming of the same. The following three deviations from the original mechanical–aggregative logic will be discussed in this chapter:

- The inclusion of assumptions regarding the imperfection of markets (in particular, with the theory of monopolistic competition).
- The introduction of possible cost of using the price mechanism (with Coase's neoinstitutionalist theses).
- The insertion of elements of uncertainty in the decisions of individuals (caused by circulating Simon's thought on bounded rationality).

The first turning point within the mechanical–aggregative method occurred with the attempt to incorporate within the original framework the functioning of *imperfect markets*. Particular reference should be made to the studies by Edward Chamberlin (1933, 1937, 1951) on "monopolistic competition" and by Joan Robinson (1933, 1934, 1953) on "imperfect competition." In the perfectly competitive markets, to which the neoclassical theoreticians refer, the demand curve of each producer is parallel to the x axis: this means that the price, indicated on the y axis, is always the same, irrespective of the quantities sold. It is the underlying hypothesis that makes producers "price takers": they cannot change the price without causing the cancellation of their products' purchases (in other words, there is total demand elasticity concerning price). This happens because the products are perfectly homogeneous. In contrast, in a monopoly, the demand curve of the monopolist coincides with that of the market (it decreases as the price increases). The monopolist vendor may therefore decide the price or quantity: in the case of the former, the market will establish what quantity to buy at what price; in the last case, the market will decide at what price that quantity can be purchased. In contrast, in the system of monopolistic competition, although there remains the hypothesis of a plurality of vendors, firms sell goods that are similar but not perfectly substitutable. The demand curve of the vendors will therefore not be flat like that of vendors in a system of perfect competition, nor will it correspond to that of the monopolist. There is a certain degree of substitution but imperfect elasticity. In the approach of the first theoreticians of imperfect markets, firms have a certain range of maneuvers to working on product differentiation: they can advertise their goods or change their offer, creating differential values concerning other suppliers. The first theories on imperfect markets, which then opened the way to a very fertile strand of economic thought, clearly showed the significance of deviation of the paradigm toward complexity. The theoreticians who brought about this turning point worked with the same instruments (demand and supply curves, marginal revenues and costs, etc.) and with the same cognitive objectives (market price determination and equilibrium definition) as their theorizing ancestors but sought to insert into the theoretical reference framework an element of complexity that they noted in real markets: the existence of distorting mechanisms of competition, namely, the nonperfect substitutability of goods among themselves. This seemingly simple difference, however, raises questions about certain basic elements of the paradigm: if the price is no longer the only variable of demand functions, each product will have a different demand curve, and hence, the curves will no longer be summable. Furthermore, the field opens up hypotheses of the interdependence of behavior (competitors will look reciprocally at differentiation actions), and the hypothesis of perfect mobility entering and exiting markets (which is indispensable to ensure the homeostatic return to equilibrium) falls away.

A second turning point in the mechanical–aggregative model came from the analysis made by Ronald Coase (Nobel Prize for Economics in 1991) in his essay *The Nature of the Firm* (1937), which opened the path to the neoinstitutionalist strand[2] and the formulation of the transaction costs theory, later developed by Williamson (1981, 1986). Here too, the deviation may be considered as coming from within the original framework insofar as the author—albeit under the influence of his studies of law—was a keen scholar of Marshallian analysis. In reality, when Coase wrote the above work, he had no intention of writing a text on

[2] According to some (Landreth & Colander, 1994, pp. 388–389), institutionalism theorists can be divided into three movements: a) traditional institutionalist economics, of which Veblen, Mitchell, and Commons are a part; b) the quasi-institutionalists, more non-conformists, although supporters of a large part of the institutionalist positions, including great economists such as Schumpeter and Galbraith; c) the neo-institutionalism, a strand that takes its cue from the work of Coase and continues mainly thanks to the work of Williamson.

transaction costs—a term that he would not even use in his essay[3]—but sought to explain the proliferation of firms that had different characteristics from the anonymous producers envisioned by neoclassical analysis.[4] Under the marginalist hypothesis, the market processed trade optimally and the cost of using the market (transaction cost) was zero. In other words, no costs were envisioned for searching for information, negotiating the contract, and its correct execution. In his analysis, Coase stated that firms arise and develop because in reality, it is not always true that the cost of using the market is zero, and in some cases, bringing trade within the firm may be less expensive than managing the same with an external transaction. Dignity is thus assumed by the internal hierarchy as an institution able to process the exchange as an alternative to the market, hence the term neoinstitutionalist given to this research strand. The firm will grow to the point at which the operations are still worth performing, while some transactions will continue to be undertaken on the outside since there is a decreasing performance of the entrepreneurial function. This may happen because of the rise in the cost of organizing new transactions within the firm or because it may be cheaper to use smaller firms. Hence, firms develop in different ways, and each presents completely individual dimensions and characteristics: despite retaining transaction and price as fundamental elements of the original paradigm, Coase's analysis presented a firm, which is already an organized system, within which differentiated transactions are carried out and which therefore approaches specific organizational configurations. Coase sought to deal with transactions within the firm with the same conceptual instruments as transactions occurring in the market, thus seeking to bring the study of organizations within the neoclassical methodology. Inevitably, however, his analysis imposed a powerful deviation upon the original framework, as it is clear the individual identity of each organization and the parallel impossibility of aggregating their behavior based on linear functions.

[3] Coase will use the term "transaction costs" only in a subsequent article, "The Problem of Social Cost" (1960), whereas the 1937 article speaks of "cost of using the price mechanism" (Coase, 1937).

[4] He himself stated later on that when he wrote *The Nature of the Firm* he was a young man who knew little about Economics and had introduced the category of transaction costs to explain the emergence of the firm (Coase, 1988, p. 35).

A third turning point in the mechanical–aggregative theoretical perspective lies in the insertion of uncertainty and *bounded rationality* into decision models. The input for this shift comes from a stimulus outside the underlying framework and, as stated above, should be ascribed to the spread of theories on bounded rationality, which, starting from the late 1940s, was chiefly thanks to the work of Herbert Simon (among others, 1947, 1955, 1976, 1979). The development of behavioral sciences, within which Simon's work in many ways may be included, does not fall within the original paradigm of marginalist microeconomics. However, the subsequent developments in economics studies had to take into account the conceptual advances that occurred in describing rationality.

In opposition to the model of full subjective rationality, which underpinned marginalist microeconomics, Simon proposed a model of satisfactory choice. Individuals cannot know all the possible alternatives, with a result associated with each of them, and with a utility function associated with each possible result. Rather, the individual has a certain "aspiration level" and selects from the set of choices those that satisfy the level in question. In this context, a substantial role is played by the time factor: while in the optimal choice model all information is available for free simultaneously, in reality, the search for information occurs in sequence (procedural rationality). Hence, if the time available is expanded, a greater number of alternatives can be explored, but the cost of the search increases, such that the behavior that extends the raft of possibilities is not necessarily a more rational behavior. Time also determines the history of decision processes, which is why the choice on a given occasion also depends on the results of choices made in previous moments.

The introduction of bounded rationality within the basic framework should be considered a turning point and not as a new paradigm insofar as Simon proposed that decision processes remain, at least in the intention, rational, distancing themselves from the extreme theses sometimes advocated by Psychology, which in some cases consider decisions driven by purely emotional motivations. Furthermore, despite weakening the model of rationality, Simon did not forgo measurements through complex mathematical tools, which chiefly use the calculation of probability.

However, the insertion of uncertainty and imperfect information in decision systems weakened several basic tenets of marginalist microeconomic theory, which was based on the assumption of perfect knowledge and the optimization of preference evaluation processes. The revisiting of *Homo Oeconomicus* after the spread of theories on weak rationality marks a turning point in marginalist theory: subsequent Microeconomics would insert uncertainty and attempt to incorporate the sequentiality and interdependence of behavior into choice models.

3.3 The Causal–Structuralist Theoretical Perspective

Industrial Organization is chiefly responsible for having focused the study of the task environment on the industrial sector (industry), following the initial tracks of the Marshallian framework on partial equilibrium. Without lingering on the definitional possibilities of industry, it should be pointed out that the Industrial Organization arose from the need to bring back the analysis of the micro, meso, and macro relationships onto a terrain of greater adherence to reality, limiting a reference context probably more homogeneous (in terms of commodity, technology, and/or geography) than the abstract neoclassical market.

Within the discipline termed Industrial Organization, the *causal–structuralist* approach is clear in the lecture that the Harvard school gives to micro, meso, and macro relationships through the Structure–Conduct–Performance (S–C–P) paradigm (Bain, 1950, 1951, 1956, 1968; Caves, 1964; Mason, 1939, 1949). This justifies the term used to define this approach, namely, causal–structuralist. Indeed, it is an interpretation based on the monodirectional *causal* nexus (such was the original paradigm) between the *structure* of the industry (reference macrocontext), the company's potential for discretionary maneuvers, and hence the firm's possibility of making extra profits.

This interpretation should also be historically contextualized. On the one hand, economic analysts felt the need to create space for market imperfection conditions, which, from the 1930s to the 1960s, were evident features of industrial contexts. On the other hand, as a subject of economic analysis, the firm radically changed. The undifferentiated producers of the neoclassical economics had been replaced by complex organizations, often of a considerable size, with distinctive individual characteristics. The objectives of oligopolistic firms, as seen by industrial economists, were complex, and profit was to be achieved through several specific subobjectives: promoting growth, preventing entry into the market of new competitors, or agreeing on collusive maneuvers.

The observations made by the Harvard school implicitly associated the oligopolistic situation of the sectors (structure) with the collusive behavior of firms (conduct), which allowed extra profits to be made (performance). This conceptual context produced an articulate theory on sector entry conditions and barriers preventing such entry.

In methodological terms, this interpretation of the micro, meso, and macro relationships is based on a great weight of empirical verification and attempts to include the interdependence of firms' behavior within the inquiry. However, the methodological differences are not only due to the changed conditions of the context in question but also due to the different cognitive objectives of the discipline. The industrial economists of Harvard aimed to understand whether, through appropriate political economy maneuvers, a distorted allocation of resources could be avoided. Starting from the premise that oligopolistic collusion led to the alteration of market mechanisms, the inquiries of the Harvard school sought to ascertain whether, intervening upstream on structures of industrial sectors, it was possible in some way to affect the mechanisms determining extra profit downstream. In this sense, the aim was to create a system of *workable competition* (Clark, 1940), that is, a competition structure that could be pursued in real markets. The causal–structuralist approach for interpreting the micro, meso, and macro relationships greatly affected antitrust regulation policies that developed in the US in those years and that sought to reduce the power of the large US corporations to favor a democratic process of entrepreneurship, in line with the idea of a pluralist society in which individuals could fulfill their aspirations.

3.3.1 Turning Points in the Causal–Structuralist Theoretical Perspective

In the causal–structuralist approach, some turning points may be identified. In particular, three examples[5] of moments of deviation have been identified: without leading to a decisive reversal, these have in some way allowed the integration and/or evolution of the interpretation of the micro, meso, and macro relationships toward theoretical principles explaining a part of the complexity that had not been decoded by the original framework. All three of these moments of change revisit the role of the company within the structuralist scheme in some form, acknowledging, from various points of view, greater discretion of the same in the relationship with its reference context. The said moments of change are the following:

- The possibility of retroaction of the structure–conduct–performance paradigm (with which the likelihood of more complex bidirectional relationships between the members of the paradigm is admitted).
- The possibility of breaking sectoral boundaries in the competition analysis and the consequent admission for competitive purposes of potential overlaps between different industries.
- The reinterpretation of the theory of barriers in a double sense: on the one hand, accepting that barriers affect companies in different ways (due to the differences between companies belonging to the same industry but also the differences between new potential entrants) and, on the other hand, recognizing that, in some cases, what we are used to representing as barriers to entry can become preferential access routes (thus playing an exact opposite role to that established by the previous theory).

The first significant deviation toward complexity is obtained if the possibility of *retroaction of the S–C–P paradigm* is admitted. In other words,

[5] As said concerning mechanical–aggregative logic, the turning points described in this chapter appear to be the most significant ones, and yet, they must be considered examples and probably do not exhaust the potential theoretical deviations manifested within the causal–structuralist theoretical perspective.

we begin to observe that not only does the structure of the industrial sector affects the conduct of the firm and hence its performance but that, in contrast, there can also be bidirectional relationships between the members of the paradigm (the conduct of firms, if accompanied by satisfactory performance, affects the configuration of the industry). In reality, the analyses of Harvard economists already indicate the effect of business strategies on the morphology of the industrial sector: an obvious example consists of the collusive maneuvers of incumbents to prevent access to new entrants, which result in (or, at any rate, accentuate) the oligopolistic nature of the industry.

In the most widespread formulation of this evolution, the main sequence, identifying the original causal nexus (structure–conduct–performance), is completed with a secondary sequence (performance–conduct–structure), which identifies the retroactive effect. According to other models, the scheme assumes a circular organization that does not identify a hierarchy of sequences but also inserts other variables such as the reinvestment of profit and the influence of firm behavior upon sector demand (Martin, 1994).

Here we have a good example of a turning point, a clear attempt to take on board the complexity of the phenomenon without rejecting the initial paradigm. There is a desire to salvage the idea that there exists a meso-economic space defined as the industrial sector, but at the same time, it is admitted that such a space cannot be determined *a priori*, regardless of the behavior of the firms operating within it. Rather, it appears evident that firms' conduct also affects sectoral design. This means implicitly introducing a coevolutionary relationship of the company concerning the reference context, which remained excluded from the cause–effect connection expected using the initial approach.

Also well known is Porter's *five forces model* (1980), and all the theories, which, in its wake, have in some way broken down the sector's traditional confines, represent a turning point compared to the original structural approach. This move toward complexity seeks, in particular, to combine sectoral with strategic analysis, spawning a particular strand of the theory of a competitive advantage (which then also finds room in the strategic–competitive approach[6]). Porter, who trained at Harvard in a cultural

[6] See Sect. 3.4.

background very close to that of Industrial Organization, attempted to incorporate within sectoral analysis the complexity that he found in the business world. As a consultant for many large public and private firms, Porter realized that the traditional confines of real competition (the firms that at a certain time produce the same goods or services) did not exhaustively define the extent of competition and that the average profit rates in industries were also influenced by other phenomena such as the threat of new entrants, the contractual power held by suppliers and customers along the supply chains, and the potential of competition from substitute products. With his five forces scheme, Porter thus structured that the sector's tendential rate of profit, measured by the long-term return on capital invested by the firms, does not only depend on the behavior of the firms involved in the sector.

However, Porter, in an attempt to save the sectoral dimension of competition, in some way abandoned the original scheme because he extends competitive boundaries thus far as to make the industry, as the meso-economic unit of reference, lose its original identity. The enlarged forces of competition deprive the new identified space (this sort of extended sector) of product limitations (insofar as products experience competition from substitutes), the time limit (competition does not only apply to firms currently on the market), and of the vertical boundaries defined at the level of the supply chain stage as the analysis is verticalized upstream and downstream (suppliers and customers). Porter indefinitely expanded the limits of the original sector, leaving firms the task of limiting the area of strategic interest: he stated that the firms themselves would be the ones to decide in which "business area" to compete, opening the way to a reference context that would become part of the competition strategy approach in which Porter ended up converging. However, the circumstances described in some way overturn the original scheme of structuralist explanation. It is not the firm that moves in a limited field of maneuver defined by the structure of the industrial sector; rather, the firm defines its macrocontext reference in a broad sectoral view.

A third turning point within the causal–structuralist approach may be seen in *theories that revisit the original theory of barriers* proposed by Bain. This theory distinguished between potential new entrants and incumbents (firms already present in the sector): the latter in some cases enjoyed a privileged position due to the higher costs incurred by new entrants to gain access to the market, with no explicit difference being made among different incumbents and among different new entrants.

Also in this circumstance, the shift toward complexity arises from those who had studied and worked within the structuralist school and who had in some way absorbed the culture of the theory of entry conditions: this theory constituted a key element in the industrialist approach that had been developed in Harvard. The theory on barriers evolved thanks to two major theoretical contributions: the article *From Entry Barriers to Mobility Barriers: Conjectural Decisions and Contrived Deterrence to New Competition* by Caves and Porter (1977) and *Gateways to Entry* by Yip (1982), reproposed in a later book by the same author (Yip, 1982).

Caves and Porter highlighted the concept of mobility barriers within the sector: the latter is not compact on the inside but is divided into strategic groups (of firms), which are homogeneous in terms of strategic behavior. Given that, barriers depend not only on structural industry elements but also on the behavior of competitors. The differences in competitive attitudes among the latter means that not all firms are equally protected within the sector (there is not a "collective performance" of the firms in the industry). Hence, entry is not the same throughout the industry, and sequential entries can be imagined, entailing an initial entry into strategic groups that are easier to penetrate (fringe) and subsequent shifts into more protected areas (core).

Instead, Yip's publications hypothesize that the traditionally privileged position for incumbents may be translated into an advantageous condition for new entrants. Hence, his idea is that barriers may translate into "gateways." Indeed, unlike Bain, Yip included already existing firms among the potential new entrants and observed that they may possess assets and skills that can invalidate the negative consequences of barriers or weaken the reactions of firms already present. Advantages may arise if businesses are correlated, which allows synergies and economies of scale to be exploited, or if new firms can exploit technological or marketing innovations, which allow incumbents to be attacked from the side, outcompeting them strategically.

These evolutions of the theories of barriers appear to be turning points in the original theory. While seeking to save their basic framework, they attempt to incorporate the current complexity, thus eliminating a few major premises of the original theory. The theory of internal mobility, for example, arises with the attempt to explain why in the sector there are different profit rates for different firms, albeit still referring to the same industry. In the current fact, the theory of strategic groups (and the consequent hypothesis of the existence of mobility barriers within the sector) explains the existence of discrepancies in the rates of return on capital invested by strategically heterogeneous firms but breaks the compactness of the sector. It becomes more difficult in such circumstances to reconstruct whether the diversity between firms should be ascribed to differences in groupings within the sector itself or whether, instead, the boundaries of industry are broken, entering the perimeter of another. We are now in a sector that no longer has external boundaries but also has deep internal differentiations. The granite block of the industrial sector has become a shadow of its former self, and it is increasingly difficult to recognize a definite mesoeconomic unit for the purpose of comparison in empirical analyses.

In conclusion, in the above shifts, the barriers no longer appear as collective goods that act structurally for all existing firms but are linked to the individual company behavior and as such generate asymmetric advantages, driving this strand toward an evidently strategist drift.

3.4 The Strategic–Competitive Theoretical Perspective

The strategic–competitive theoretical perspective to interpreting micro, meso, and macro relationships arose after the 1950s within US business schools and was later extended, with different approaches, to Europe and other parts of the world. The firm is positioned at the center of the knowledge process: it interprets, by using the strategy, its reference environment, although without ever achieving perfect mastery of it. In this approach, external reality does not seem able to be dominated. Indeed, it is precisely the opacity of the environmental context that leads to the development of a particular entrepreneurial ability: that of deciphering the context in which the firm operates, seeking to maximize its potential for success (strategy). The difference in the *strategic* ability of competitors generates behavioral asymmetries in the *competition* process and makes each firm different from the others, hence the *strategic–competitive* term to identify the approach to the micro, meso, and macro relationships.

Based on this way of thinking, the environmental variables are opaque, and it is the top management of the company (or whoever the strategic subject is) that interprets them, thereby giving impetus to competitive action, while the context is redefined restrictively, depending on the elements the company is directly interested in. This produces new mesoeconomic dimensions, such as the "strategic business area" that presents more nuanced boundaries (circumscribed according to the strategic needs of the company) than the environment of neoclassical or industrial economists.

Also on this occasion, the approach suffers from its position in history. The ability to choose the strategy of the great US firms of the period seems to suggest that the invisible hand of the market was replaced by the visible hand of management (Chandler, 1977, p. 1), a powerful new social category. The US capitalism in the 1960s not only put the firm and the reference environment on the same plan, but it seems to have attributed to large firms—"the most powerful institution in the American economy" (Chandler, 1977, p. 1)—the power to determine the connotations of the industries in which they operate.

The firm leveraged its power using complex analytical tools with which the managerial class prepared to take on the challenges of the environmental context. It was a strongly normative, specialist approach, and studies were highly pragmatically organized. Indeed, it is no coincidence that in this context, the standard teaching methodology was based on company case studies. The great variety of contributions, the absence of a dominant paradigm, and the blending of functional analysis with contributions from Industrial Organization make it very difficult to identify a clear theoretical basis for the discipline. A common pattern may be seen in the original "formulation/implementation paradigm" typical of strategic planning, which clearly distinguished the phase of strategy design from that of its execution. The detailed instrumentation required to tackle the process of strategy formulation and implementation is described in some fundamental contributions of strategic analysis (among others

Andrews, 1971; Ansoff, 1965; Hofer & Schendel, 1978) and supported by models set up by large consulting firms, such as product portfolio matrix by the Boston Consulting Group (1972) or the 7S scheme by McKinsey (Peters & Waterman, 1982; Waterman et al., 1980).

Into the strategist strand flowed other contributions from previous approaches. The strategic–competitive theoretical perspective, for example, embraced the Porterian developments of structuralist analysis, progress in the neoinstitutionalist analysis made by Williamson (1975, 1981) based on the original input from Coase, and in-depth studies of theories on bounded rationality that inserted processes related to uncertainty and experimentation into firms' strategy study (among others Cyert & March, 1963; Cohen et al., 1972; Nelson & Winter, 1982). Furthermore, the strategic–competitive approach was often contaminated by organizational theories of adaptation. Analysis of organizational structures that were better suited to environmental conditions was studied, for instance, by contingency theory (among others, Burns & Stalker, 1961; Lawrence & Lorsch, 1967).

3.4.1 Turning Points in the Strategic–Competitive Theoretical Perspective

Even the strategic–competitive theoretical perspective has seen a change in its approach over time to get closer and closer to a vision of the micro, meso, and macro relationships that is compatible with complexity. The company is recognized as having discriminatory power in the original competitive framework to select the reference context in which the greatest opportunities nestle and to analyze and address the processes of adaptation to the environment. The prerequisite of the original framework lies in the fact that the strategic process can adjust the connection of the strengths and weaknesses of the company with the system of threats–opportunities found in the market. Over time, this approach has become a coevolutionary conception of the business–environment relationship, in which the original process of adaptation has gradually been accompanied by a cogenerative process of external reality, which companies contribute to determining.

The four turning points toward complexity are those in which the following are observed:

- Dignity is given to spontaneity and emergency in the strategic process, depending on the circumstances that were coproduced in the micro, meso, and macro relationships.
- It was the company that created its reference environment, according to its own needs: reference to this logic, for example, is made by the "definition of the business" as a strategic moment, functional to the specific needs of a company and modifiable according to the visions of competitors (Abell, 1980).
- New plural competitive systems were introduced (networks, districts, populations) that could be placed in the meso-economy, halfway between the microeconomic dimension and the macroeconomic dimension.
- The value of resources (resource-based view), the importance of dynamic capabilities, and the firm's knowledge was placed alongside market positioning as a source of competitive advantage.

The 1970s may symbolically be viewed as the years in which the original formulation/implementation paradigm and all its structured baggage began to be questioned by management scholars. The 1970s marked a break in the long period of economic development, which had continued almost uninterruptedly since the end of World War II and which had witnessed the progressive emergence of mass markets. In economic terms, several major events left their mark on the period: the fall of the currency system established with the Bretton Woods agreement, the great oil crises, and inflationary phenomena with concomitant stagnation elements. In this changing scenario, management studies allow for the growing complexity of the micro, meso, and macro relationships, seeking from several standpoints to incorporate such complexity. The four turning points in the strategic–competitive theoretical perspective are identified above.

The first shift may be observed in the theories, which began abandoning *the plan as a guiding element in business strategy*: the entrepreneurial visions theorized by Normann (1977), the "emerging strategies" defined by Mintzberg (1978), and "logical incrementalism" hypothesized by Quinn (1980, 1981) are all works in which the possibility of determining *a priori* the strategic path of a company based on planning is in some way rejected. Normann (1977, p. 49) imagines that sometimes planners do not develop objectives as future states to pursue but rather act based on a view, deciding only the first states of a process. Through his research into several case studies, Mintzberg found that the strategy used may come not only from intentionally developed decisions but also from contingent and occasional choices and that there are often reverse processes by which subsequent implementation affects the formulation, generating changes in the latter *in itinere* (emerging strategies). Quinn explained the results recorded on a sample of ten firms according to logical incrementalism, which often steers decision-making processes. Only some of the main actions are predefined, whereas most of the activities are determined *in itinere*, often under urgent or unforeseen circumstances.

Although they may be seen as a continuation of strategic management studies, these theories reject that the planning philosophy behind the original strategic studies could be applied to all firms. This has led to several consequences. First, the prescriptive weight of this strand of studies was weakened: the first version of this framework was strongly anchored to analytical tools that were supposed to serve management as a guide to be able to commit its activity. Evidently, at the moment when the circumstances of activities could no longer be determined *a priori* but became clear *in itinere* and in a contingent fashion, it became less useful to use prescriptive schemes of behavior. Furthermore, what emerged more clearly was the hypothesis of a subjective interpretation of the micro, meso, and macro relationships, which is decoded individually and personally according to the specific operating circumstances of the firm and its management.

A second turning point in the strategic–competitive approach may be considered the revision of the environmental dimension of the relationship, through the *definition of business*, as proposed by Abell (1980). The well-known three-dimensional scheme definitively abandons the traditional units of demand and supply, breaking them down into three dimensions: "technologies," "customer groups," and "customer needs." It consciously abandoned any sector characterization of the reference context and focused on a more useful functional parameter (customer needs) to study competition. The parallel combination with technology, on the one hand, and customer groups, on the other, broadly recovers elements of the economic tradition, albeit applying them much more flexibly. The logic of the micro, meso, and macro relationships compared with that described by the S–C–P paradigm was overturned when Abell declared that the market remains delimited by the sum of business defined by competitors over a certain period. The reference context becomes the sum of what, at a certain moment, competitors express as the overall result of their strategic choices. It thus expands, shrinks, or changes continuously according to the competitive decisions of the individual actors.

Further, we may note both the continuity and break with the original paradigm. The hereditary line is ensured by the search for a unit of environmental inquiry, which is useful for studying competition. In this sense, the business designed by Abell is a formidable tool representing the reference area of interest for the firm. The lack of continuity may be found in the limit to which Abell takes his analysis: a reference environment that no longer exists as such but only because it is imagined as this by firms.

A further shift involved the revisitation of the other element in the relation: the firm. Indeed, there has been increased interest in *sets of firms*, which are in some way homogeneous and which could be of greater interest than individual units for strategic–competitive analysis. A very prolific current of thought is dedicated to firms, which in some way manage cooperative relations (among others, Contractor & Lorange, 1988; Johanson & Mattsson, 1987; Miles & Snow, 1986, 1992). We are referring to studies on "networks" between companies that share strategic relationships. A current of thought also explored the characteristics of "industrial districts" (among others, Piore & Sabel, 1984), in which groups of firms share the same geographical area and social fabric, in addition to having economic links. Another current, of a primarily organizational stamp, focuses on studying "populations," organizations that have structural affinities (Hannan & Freeman, 1977, 1984). For reasons of space, it is impossible to run through the complex literature that lies behind these significant shifts. The aim here is simply to underline both elements of congruence and aspects of deviation in these studies compared with the original strategic–competitive model.

All these theories in some way belong to the strategic approach because they repropose the basic characteristics of this scheme to explain the micro, meso, and macro relationships: there is an environment to interpret with suitable formulas to operate competitively within it. Also the population ecology theory, which lends itself to such an interpretation less than the other two, may be included in this approach whose cultural environment it shares; suffice it to think of the description of r-strategies/k-strategies or the definition of generalists and specialists in niche theory (Hannan & Freeman, 1977, 1984).

The elements of deviation appear equally obvious. Micro has ceased to be a single actor (the firm), becoming a plural entity (the network, district, or also a population with specific structural characteristics), a new unit of inquiry, which raises competition to a different level. These new aggregates generate complex effects insofar as they are not only the sum of the units that make them up: they are not organizationally integrated like the large corporations described by Chandler, but neither are they autonomously independent like marginalist producers. In these circumstances, once again, the administration of a plan from the core or from the top becomes more difficult. Again, laying down lines of action defined *a priori* becomes problematic because the interactions established within the plural organism are guided not only by coordination but also by local sensitivities.

The fourth example of deviation from the original strategic–competitive approach lies in the strand originating with the contributions of the *resource-based view* (Barney, 1986, 1991; Dierickx & Cool, 1989; Grant, 1991; Rumelt, 1984; Wernerfelt, 1984, 1995), continues with subsequent analyses of the concepts of *core competencies* (Prahalad & Hamel, 1990), *capabilities* (Amit & Schoemaker, 1993), *dynamic capabilities* (Teece & Pisano, 1994; Teece et al., 1997) and is completed with the parallel strand of the *knowledge-based view* (among others, Boisot, 1998; Davenport & Prusak, 2000; Kogut & Zander, 1992; Nonaka, 1994; Nonaka & Takeuchi, 1995; Spender & Grant, 1996; von Krogh et al., 2000; Tsoukas, 1996; Zander & Kogut, 1995). All the above contributions, differing in many ways, are assimilated by the willingness to find within the firm a key to interpreting the great strategic theme of competitive advantage. In some ways, it is a varied strand of a purely strategist response to the progress of competitive advantage obtained from industrialists that, with Porter's analyses, has long dominated the area of strategic competitive studies. While pursuing the strategic–competitive intent is evident, it should be explained why such studies are thought to represent a turning point *vis-à-vis* the initial paradigm. According to the contributions in question, the firm must concentrate on its resources, skills, and knowledge rather than on its market positioning to be able to achieve success. To obtain a competitive advantage, the firm should not so much look at placement in the industry as its endowment of differential resources, able to create innovation and deal with a very dynamic environment.

* * *

What we affirm here is that, over time, we have noticed in each theoretical perspective the need to make the analyses more consonant with the complexity found in the phenomenical reality. This indicates, as will also be argued below, not a progressive approach to increasingly complete knowledge but rather the awareness of mutual contamination of different logics, historically determined but theoretically susceptible to incessant evolutions and reciprocal propagations.

In this sense, the proposal presented in the following chapters is one of the possible efforts to interpret complexity.

3.5 The Characteristics of Decision-Making Processes in the Various Theoretical Perspectives

From the point of view of management studies, one of the most stimulating aspects of the reconstruction we presented is the impact in terms of decision-making processes. The distinct configuration of the micro, meso, and macro relationships leads to a different interpretation of the decision-making processes that occur within the company and, consequently, also of the meaning of the leadership by the top management. The theme will be taken up in Chap. 6, when the interpretation of the role of the command in the representation of the micro, meso, and macro relationships in terms of complexity will be clearer. Here, we only wish to provide a first brief overview of the implications, in terms of decision-making processes, deriving from the adoption of one of the three theoretical perspectives analyzed (and the subsequent deviations toward complexity) to complete the reading of the interpretative paths presented.

3.5.1 Mechanical–Aggregative Theoretical Perspective

According to this interpretation, the relationship with the macro is kept perfectly under control by the subjects appointed to make decisions. There is no uncertainty about the options that affect performance: the decision-making process is guided by the objective of optimizing the variables on which one can operate (e.g., choosing between alternative factors of production) and is guaranteed by the perfect rationality of the actors (consumers and producers). Variables out of the control of operators are considered data (technology) or are generated by the mechanical combination of relationships between economic actors (price). As we have seen, in subsequent advancements concerning the original approach, the decision logic is based on the interdependence and the imperfect rationality of behavior. In these positions, the computability of the effects related to decisions becomes more nuanced, the aspiration to optimal evaluations is abandoned to turn toward satisfactory options, and the possibility of procedural rationality is admitted, based on a process of trial and error.

3.5.2 Causal–Structuralist Theoretical Perspective

The degree of domination of events, in the original framework, on the part of the strategic top management is limited to the restricted options left to the conduct of companies within a potentially homogeneous context (the industry). Some variables cannot be easily influenced (the given conditions of the sector) and decision-making processes are conditioned by the structural attributes of the reference context (industry). As said, subsequent advancements consider broadened definitions of competitive contexts and the possibility of retroactivity on the industry's connotations of companies' actions; in some formulations, the vision of barriers is reversed, which could become an invitation for entry: obviously, these deviations increase the possibilities of maneuvering of the competitors.

3.5.3 Strategic–Competitive Theoretical Perspective

In its initial version, the emphasis—in terms of decision-making processes—was placed on the effort to predict the trends of the environmental context and to plan behavior in line with these forecasts (long-range planning). The poor defensibility of this planning attitude in conditions of opacity of the micro, meso, and macro relationships has prompted different revision processes. In almost all of the subsequent advancements, a modification of the features of strategic selection is implicit. Where total dominance is impossible, we work with experimental behaviors, and the strategic decision-making processes integrate logics that mix competition and cooperation.

3.6 Toward the Complex Systems' Theoretical Perspective

The conceptual framework provided by the theories on Luhmannian-derived social systems and using the approach developed by von Foerster and Maturana and Varela on self-organizing and autopoietic systems, along with the reflections of many authors in terms of complexity (among others, Morin, Bocchi, and Ceruti) and business–environment relationships (among others, Weick and Vicari),[7] have prompted us to draft a fourth possibility of reading the relationship between companies and industry/markets, which we have precisely defined as the complex systems' theoretical perspective. At this point, it is worth clarifying that the systemic theory has many souls, which are not always homogeneous, and

[7] Bibliographical references to the works of these authors can be found in Chaps. 4, 5, and 6.

it is therefore important to reiterate that the theoretical perspective proposed in the following chapters is inspired by a precise stage of systemic thinking, which we can define as theories on complex or self-referential systems. The interpretative perspective of micro, meso, and macro relationships contained in the following chapters was created based on the stimuli coming from this conceptualization and from the literature on complexity, as well as from some recent advancements in business theory.

The company selects some relationships concerning the infinite possibilities of experience and action and uses "meaning"[8] as a reference to new possibilities: the potential scope of reference is quite ample, precisely because the possibilities of the systemic referral are infinite.

The enterprise system defines itself as *other* in opposition to the environment, which remains circumscribed by difference: the company will undertake relationships with other systems that are part of its environment, thus activating a vision of the company–task environment relationship functional to its reproduction. As we will see, this approach will allow us to face the central nodes of scientific research on micro, meso, and macro relationships presented in Chap. 2 from a different viewpoint.

The decision-making processes in this conceptual environment must be capable of tolerating the uncertainty connected to the complexity and unawareness of the environmental reality in its entirety. Complexity becomes defining to the objects of study, and decision-making processes can only be generated within the frame of this premise. As a decision-making entity, the company, on the one hand, adapts to the complexity of the environment, and on the other hand, as it becomes increasingly complex, it contributes to changing the connotations of the context in a coevolutionary relationship that radically modifies the conceptualization of the decision-making function. It is necessary to create awareness of the self-observation process that the company (but also all the other actors in the relation) generates on itself as part of the micro, meso, and macro relationships and, consequently, on the dual role it plays as an observed system and as an observing system.

[8] As we will see in more detail later, the meaning is defined as the strategy that guides system selection operation.

References

Abell, D. F. (1980). *Defining the Business: The Starting Point of Strategic Planning.* Prentice Hall.

Amit, R., & Schoemaker, P. J. H. (1993). Strategic Assets and Organizational Rent. *Strategic Management Journal, 14*(1), 33–46.

Andrews, K. R. (1971). *The Concept of Corporate Strategy.* Homewood.

Ansoff, H. I. (1965). *Corporate Strategy.* McGraw-Hill.

Bain, J. S. (1950). Workable Competition in Oligopoly: Theoretical Considerations and Some Empirical Evidence. *American Economic Review, 40*(2), 35–47.

Bain, J. S. (1951). Relation of Profit Rate to Industry Concentration: American Manufacturing, 1936–1940. *The Quarterly Journal of Economics., 65*(3), 293–324.

Bain, J. S. (1956). *Barriers to New Competition. Their Character and Consequences in Manufacturing Industries.* Harvard University Press.

Bain, J. S. (1968). *Industrial Organization* (2nd ed.). John Wiley & Sons.

Barney, J. B. (1986). Strategic Factor Markets: Expectations, Luck, and Business Strategy. *Management Science, 32*(10), 1231–1241.

Barney, J. B. (1991). Firm Resources and Sustained Competitive Advantage. *Journal of Management, 17*(1), 99–120.

Boisot, M. H. (1998). *Knowledge Assets. Securing Competitive Advantage in the Information Economy.* Oxford University Press.

Boston Consulting Group. (1972). *Perspectives on Experience.* Boston Consulting Group Inc.

Burns, T., & Stalker, G. M. (1961). *The Management of Innovation.* Tavistock.

Caves, R. E. (1964). *American Industry: Structure, Conduct, Performance.* Prentice-Hall.

Caves, R. E., & Porter, M. E. (1977). From Entry Barriers to Mobility Barriers: Conjectural Decisions and Contrived Deterrence to New Competition. *Quarterly Journal of Economics, 91*(2), 241–261.

Chamberlin, E. H. (1933). *The Theory of Monopolistic Competition.* Harvard University Press.

Chamberlin, E. H. (1937). Monopolistic or Imperfect Competition? *The Quarterly Journal of Economics, 51*(4), 557–580.

Chamberlin, E. H. (1951). Monopolistic Competition Revisited. *Economica, 18*(72), 343–362.

Chandler, A. D., Jr. (1977). *The Visible Hand. The Managerial Revolution in American Business*. Harvard University Press.
Clark, J. M. (1940). Toward a Concept of Workable Competition. *The American Economic Review, 30*(2), 241–256.
Coase, R. H. (1937). The Nature of the Firm. *Economica, 4*(16), 386–405.
Coase, R. H. (1960). The Problem of Social Cost. *Journal of Law and Economics, 3*(1), 1–44.
Coase, R. H. (1988). The Nature of the Firm: Influence. *Journal of Law, Economics & Organization, 4*(1), 33–47.
Cohen, M. D., March, J. G., & Olsen, J. P. (1972). A Garbage Can Model of Organizational Chioce. *Administrative Science Quarterly, 17*(1), 1–25.
Contractor, F. J., & Lorange, P. (1988). *Cooperative Strategies in International Business*. Lexington Books.
Cyert, R. M., & March, J. G. (1963). *A Behavioural Theory of the Firm*. Prentice Hall.
Davenport, T. H., & Prusak, L. (2000). *Working Knowledge. How Organizations Manage What They Know*. Harvard Business Press.
Dierickx, I., & Cool, K. (1989). Asset Stock Accumulation and Sustainability of Competitive Advantage. *Management Science, 35*(12), 1504–1511.
Grant, R. M. (1991). The Resource-Based Theory of Competitive Advantage: Implications for Strategy Formulation. *California Management Review, 33*(3), 114–135.
Hannan, M. T., & Freeman, J. (1977). The Population Ecology of Organizations. *The American Journal of Sociology, 82*(5), 929–964.
Hannan, M. T., & Freeman, J. (1984). Structural Inertia and Organizational Change. *American Sociological Review, 49*(2), 149–164.
Hofer, C. H. W., & Schendel, D. (1978). *Strategy Formulation: Analytical Concepts*. West Publishing Company.
Johanson, J., & Mattsson, L. (1987). Interorganizational Relations in Industrial Systems: A Network Approach Compared with the Transaction-Cost Approach. *International Studies of Management & Organization, 17*(1), 34–48.
Kogut, B., & Zander, U. (1992). Knowledge of the Firm, Combinative Capabilities, and the Replication of Technology. *Organization Science, 3*(3), 383–397.
Landreth, H., & Colander, D. C. (1994). *History of Economic Thought*. Houghton Mifflin.
Lawrence, P. R., & Lorsch, P. R. (1967). *Organization and Environment: Managing Differentiation and Integration*. Harvard University Press.

Martin, S. (1994). *Industrial Economics. Economic Analysis and Public Policy.* Prentice Hall.
Mason, E. S. (1939). Price and Production Policies of Large-Scale Enterprise. *American Economic Review, 29*(1), 61–74.
Mason, E. S. (1949). The Current Status of the Monopoly Problem in the United States. *Harvard Law Review, 62*(8), 1265–1285.
Miles, R. E., & Snow, C. C. (1986). Organizations: New Concepts for New Forms. *California Management Review, 28*(3), 62–73.
Miles, R. E., & Snow, C. C. (1992). Causes of Failure of Network Organizations. *California Management Review, 34*(4), 53–72.
Mintzberg, H. (1978). Patterns in Strategy Formation. *Management Science, 24*(9), 934–948.
Nelson, R. R., & Winter, S. G. (1982). *An Evolutionary Theory of Economic Change.* Harvard University Press.
Nonaka, I. (1994). A Dynamic Theory of Organizational Knowledge Creation. *Organization Science, 5*(1), 14–37.
Nonaka, I., & Takeuchi, H. (1995). *The Knowledge-Creating Company How Japanese Companies Create the Dynamics of Innovation.* Oxford University Press.
Normann, R. (1977). *Management for Growth.* John Wiley & Sons.
Peters, T. J., & Waterman, R. H., Jr. (1982). *In Search of Excellence.* Harper & Row.
Piore, M. J., & Sabel, C. F. (1984). *The Second Industrial Divide. Possibilities for Prosperity.* Basic Books.
Porter, M. E. (1980). *Competitive Strategy. Techniques for Analyzing Industries and Competitors.* The Free Press.
Prahalad, C. K., & Hamel, G. (1990). The Core Competence of the Corporation. *Harvard Business Review, 68*(May–June), 79–91.
Quinn, J. B. (1980). *Strategy for Changes: Logical Incrementalism.* Irwin.
Quinn, J. B. (1981). Formulating Strategy One Step at a Time. *Journal of Business Strategy, 1*(3), 42–63.
Robinson, J. (1933). *The Economics of Imperfect Competition.* Macmillan.
Robinson, J. (1934). What Is Perfect Competition? *Quarterly Journal of Economics, 49*(1), 104–120.
Robinson, J. (1953). Imperfect Competition Revisited. *The Economic Journal, 63*(251), 579–593.
Rumelt, R. P. (1984). Towards a Strategic Theory of the Firm. In R. Lamb (Ed.), *Competitive Strategic Management.* Prentice Hall.
Simon, H. A. (1947). *Administrative Behavior. A Study of Decision-Making Processes in Administrative Organization.* Macmillan.

Simon, H. A. (1955). A Behavioral Model of Rational Choice. *Quarterly Journal of Economics, 69*(1), 99–118.

Simon, H. A. (1976). From Substantive to Procedural Rationality. In S. Latsis (Ed.), *Method and Appraisal in Economics*. Cambridge University Press.

Simon, H. A. (1979). Rational Decision Making in Business Organizations (Nobel Lecture). *American Economic Review, 69*(4), 493–513.

Spender, J. C., & Grant, R. M. (1996). Knowledge and the Firm: Overview. *Strategic Management Journal, 17*(52), 5–9.

Teece, D. J., & Pisano, G. P. (1994). The Dynamic Capabilities of Firms: An Introduction. *Industrial and Corporate Change, 3*(3), 537–556.

Teece, D. J., Pisano, G. P., & Shuen, A. (1997). Dynamic Capabilities and Strategic Management. *Strategic Management Journal, 18*(7), 509–533.

Tsoukas, H. (1996). The Firm as a Distributed Knowledge System: A Constructionist Approach. *Strategic Management Journal, 17*(52), 11–25.

von Krogh, G., Ichijo, K., & Nonaka, I. (2000). *Enabling Knowledge Creation: How to Unlock the Mystery of Tacit Knowledge and Release the Power of Innovation*. Oxford University Press.

Waterman, R. H., Jr., Peters, T. J., & Phillips, J. R. (1980). Structure Is Not Organization. *Business Horizons, 23*(3), 14–26.

Wernerfelt, B. (1984). A Resource-Based View of the Firm. *Strategic Management Journal, 5*(2), 171–180.

Wernerfelt, B. (1995). The Resource-Based View of the Firm: Ten Years After. *Strategic Management Journal, 16*(3), 171–174.

Williamson, O. E. (1975). *Market and Hierarchies: Analysis and Antitrust Implications: A Study of Internal Organization*. The Free Press.

Williamson, O. E. (1981). The Economics of Organization: The Transaction Cost Approach. *American Journal of Sociology, 87*(3), 548–577.

Williamson, O. E. (1986). *The Economic Institutions of Capitalism. Firms, Markets, Relational Contracting*. The Free Press.

Yip, G. S. (1982a). Gateways to Entry. *Harvard Business Review, 60*(5), 85–92.

Yip, G. S. (1982b). *Barriers to Entry. A Corporate-Strategy Perspective*. Lexington Books.

Zander, U., & Kogut, B. (1995). Knowledge and the Speed of the Transfer and Imitation of Organizational Capabilities: An Empirical Test. *Organization Science, 6*(1), 76–92.

4

The Micro, Meso, and Macro Relationships in Complex Systems' Theory: A Different Perspective

Abstract In this chapter we propose to examine the micro, meso, and macro relationships in Economics from the "complex systems' theoretical perspective." The idea behind this interpretative proposal is to study the links between the company and the environmental context using the framework of some systemic theses and theories on complexity. We will make express reference to the logic of autopoietic systems, with particular attention to Luhmannian thinking on social systems. It would not make sense to discuss the theory of systems in general as many different conceptualizations fall within this extensive patrimony of studies, which cannot be framed in a unitary reflection but for some basic elements.

We examine companies as complex autopoietic systems that take on significance as a function of the attempt to manage complexity and reproduce themselves. This stage of systemic thinking includes the theory developed by Luhmann regarding self-referential systems, to which, in many ways, we will refer when reviewing the micro, meso, and macro relationship in Economics. As the approach used is in line with developments in terms of self-regulatory, self-organizing, and autopoietic systems, we deemed it useful to briefly present these concepts for a better understanding of the conceptual context within which we will move.

C. Mazzoni, *Firms, Industries, Markets*, https://doi.org/10.1007/978-3-031-59823-4_4

Keywords Evolution of systemic theories toward complexity • The use of the systemic perspective in management studies • Basic concepts of Luhmannian theory on complex social systems • Complexity • Difference between system and environment • Systemic selection • Self-reference • Meaning • Systemic differentiation • Interpenetration

4.1 Evolution of Systemic Theories Toward Complexity

As mentioned, from this chapter onward, we propose to examine the micro, meso, and macro relationships in Economics from the complex systems' theoretical perspective. The idea behind this interpretative proposal is to study the links between the company and the environmental context using the framework of some systemic theses and theories on complexity. It should be immediately clarified that hereinafter, we will make express reference to the logic of autopoietic systems, with particular attention to Luhmannian thinking on social systems. It would not make sense to discuss the theory of systems in general as many different conceptualizations fall within this extensive patrimony of studies, which cannot be framed in a unitary reflection but for some basic elements:

> Today "systems theory" is a catchall concept for very different denotations and very different levels of analysis. The word refers to no unambiguous meaning. When one introduces the concept of system into sociological analyses without further clarification, then an illusory precision arises that lacks any basis. Thus, controversies arise in which one can only suppose or infer from the argumentation that the participants have different ideas in mind when they speak of systems. (Luhmann, 1995, p. 1)

Systems theory's internal evolution has substantially transformed its approach over time, including, and above all, regarding the most interesting aspect for this discussion, namely, the relationship of the system with the environment. Luhmann identified the four stages of systemic thinking described below (Fig. 4.1), highlighting a shift from an ontological

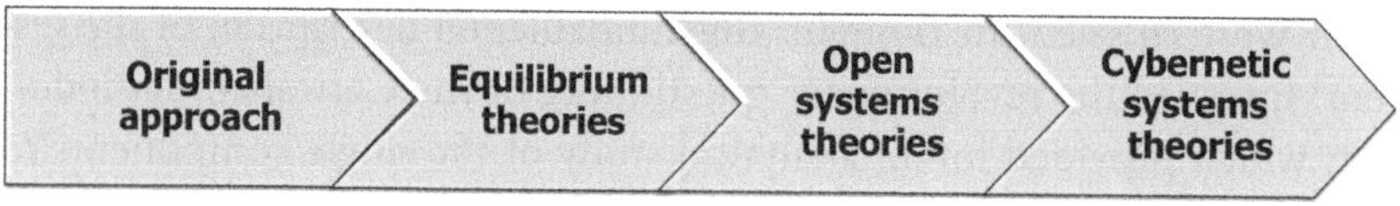

Fig. 4.1 The evolution of systems theories

There is no reference to the external environment

System ≠ Sum of its components

The specific relationship among components (organization) originates properties peculiar to the system and not to its components, that is, when we listen to a melody, we do not refer to the individual notes which form it

The sense of the whole is not obtained through analytical decomposition → rejection of Cartesian methodology

Fig. 4.2 Original approach

conception of the system toward a functional conceptualization of it, along with an ever greater reference to the relationship with the environment (Luhmann, 1969, pp. 255–256).

However, in the internal evolution of systemic thinking, the previous approaches are not denied, nor are they considered unusable, but rather, they are expanded and enriched to make them more suitable for dealing with the complexities of social reality (Luhmann, 1995, p. 5).

In the *Original approach*, the system (the whole) is seen as something different from the sum of the elements that constitute it (the parts) insomuch as the relationship in which these parts are located (the organization of the system) originates properties that belong to the system and not to the individual components. The existence of interaction between the parts makes the whole different from the sum of the elements that constitute it, allowing for the emergence of new properties of the system that cannot be traced analytically going back to the elements that form part of it. In the basic approach, the reference to the environment is of little relevance (Fig. 4.2).

In Western scientific thought, this fundamental description of the system[1] involved the revolutionary questioning of the Cartesian methodology, which provided for an analytical study of the single components to understand the meaning of the entirety (Capra, 1997, p. 29). This basic systemic approach has been exploited in many sciences. Quantum physics has shown that subatomic particles (which make up molecules and atoms) can only be interpreted as relationships and not as independent elementary units. In Psychology, Gestalt has revealed that the sensations felt when facing complex phenomena (e.g., listening to a symphony) derive from an integrated perception and not from a decomposition of the stimuli that generated it (one perceives the melody as a whole, not the individual notes). In Biology, the study of ecosystems based on food chains or communities with collective intelligence (such as bees or ants) has shown that in some ecological organizations, it is not the individual behavior that is of importance but rather the concatenation between events and the coordination between them (Capra, 1997, pp. 29–35). This approach also undermines the assumption of the neoclassical microeconomic tradition that defined the general equilibrium of markets through processes of summation of the individual behaviors of consumers and producers.

In the *Equilibrium theories*, we begin to study the relationship of the system with the environment although external influences on the system are considered sources of interference rather than constitutive factors of the system. The latter can react by absorbing them or not within its structure (Fig. 4.3).

In the *Open systems theories*, a process of constant exchange between the system and the environment is assumed. The relationship with the outside is considered a constituent element of the system and not a contingency to be eliminated (Fig. 4.4). This approach is further elaborated in the work of Ludwig von Bertalanffy (1969).

[1] This basic vision of the system as a new and diverse unit compared to the sum of its parts is frequently used in many definitions that refer to subsequent evolutions of the theory (see, among others, Morin, 2007, p. 27; Rullani & Vicari, 1999, p. 8).

Negative relationship with the environment

The system has to adapt itself according to environmental interference

↓

External influences on the system are considered sources of interference rather than factors making up the system, which can react by absorbing them—or not—within its own structure

Fig. 4.3 Equilibrium theories

Positive relationship with the environment

Constant exchange between system and environment. Relationship with the outside world is considered an element making up the system and not a matter to eliminate

Fig. 4.4 Open systems theories

As we will see better later, in *Cybernetic systems theory*,[2] the relationship between system and environment is explained mainly in terms of different complexity (the environment has degrees of complexity that cannot be fully acknowledged by the system). To relate to the environment, the system is forced both to increase its internal complexity and simultaneously to improve its selection processes, which allows it to limit the relationship to only a part of the potential complexity. In this setting, the systemic purpose is linked to the necessity of surviving within the complexity of the pertinent reference environment (Fig. 4.5).

[2] In the subsequent discussion, cybernetic theories will include the theories on complex autopoietic systems.

Constitutive relationship with the environment

Environmental complexity is considered a starting point: the system emerges as an organization in response to excessive environmental complexity

The complexity outside the system is the excess of possibilities of experiencing the world: the system reduces the external complexity, selecting only some stimuli from the outside (systemic selection)

The system, in its attempt to cope with external complexity, organizes itself, becoming ever more complex on the inside (internal differentiation) as well

Fig. 4.5 Cybernetic systems theories

By developing this latter orientation, we examine companies as complex autopoietic systems that take on significance as a function of the attempt to manage complexity and reproduce themselves (in this sense, we move toward a functional vision of the system). This last stage of systemic thinking includes the theory developed by Luhmann regarding self-referential systems, to which, in many ways, we will refer later when reviewing the micro, meso, and macro relationship in Economics (moving away from the more widespread conception of the company as an open system). As the approach used is in line with developments in terms of self-regulatory, self-organizing, and autopoietic systems, we deemed it useful to briefly present these concepts for a better understanding of the conceptual context within which we will move.

We can introduce the theories on autopoietic systems by recalling the debate between von Neumann and Wiener regarding heteronomous and autonomous systems. Von Neumann was mainly interested in the former, determined from the outside, while Wiener was more inclined toward the study of autonomous systems, determined from the inside. The debate focused on two fundamental dimensions (Varela, 2007, pp. 131–132): the characterization of the system and its relationship with the surrounding environment. Heteronomous systems are distinguished by an input–output flow and relate externally through a representation of the environment. Autonomous systems are characterized by an operational closure and behaviors that are substantially directed toward the system itself (self-behaviors). In such systems, the relationship with the environment takes place through an internal production of the external world.

While not wanting to radicalize the logical opposition between the two concepts, the theories within which we frame our description of the micro, meso, and macro relationship interpret the company as an autonomous type of system and in particular an autopoietic system.

However, to better understand the meaning of autopoiesis in systemic theory (the theme will be widely taken up below), it is worth clarifying some preliminary steps in logical order.

First, it is necessary to share the idea that systems with feedback effects, the output of which becomes the input of the system itself in subsequent cycles, can be induced to self-regulate and consequently produce a form of learning. In other words, the system learns.

The immune system of vertebrate animals is an example of a self-learning mechanism. When a bacterium or virus intervenes in an organism, it tends to multiply to the detriment of healthy cells. These pathogens are numerous, and the organism does not possess the antibodies necessary to fight them all, but it does possess a certain number of primary types formed during the development of the organism itself (a sort of basic repertoire). When attacked by a virus or bacterium, the system selects the antibody that best opposes it, making it reproduce and proliferate selectively (secondary repertoire). At the next attack by the same pathogen, there will be many antibodies capable of protecting the organism, which has learned to defend itself from that specific disturbing event.

The first conceptual step is therefore that which leads us to the identification of self-regulatory systems capable of learning following repeated observations. This constant interpretation carried out by the system on the surrounding environment and its action within it (cognitive function) allows for further consideration. The self-learning system also has a reflexive property of self-observation, self-assessment, and self-knowledge. As a result, it also performs a cognitive function toward itself, or rather, it interprets the surrounding environment and itself according to its cognitive capacity.

The next step leads us to analyze the process of self-organization of systems, studied, among others, by Ross Ashby (1962) and Heinz von Foerster (2003).

Self-organizing systems direct their energies toward organizing themselves: they are capable of diminishing their internal entropy at the expense of the entropy of the environment that surrounds them. Below are some concepts of the relationship with which von Foerster opened the Interdisciplinary Symposium on Self-Organizing Systems in Chicago on May 5, 1959, arguing that organizing systems are, in reality, disorganizing systems as they increase internal order by generating disorder in their reference environment:

> Assume a finite universe, U_0, as small or as large as we wish (Fig. 4.6), which is enclosed in an adiabatic shell which separates this finite universe from any "meta-universe" in which it may be immersed. Assume, furthermore, that in this universe, U_0, there is a closed surface which divides this

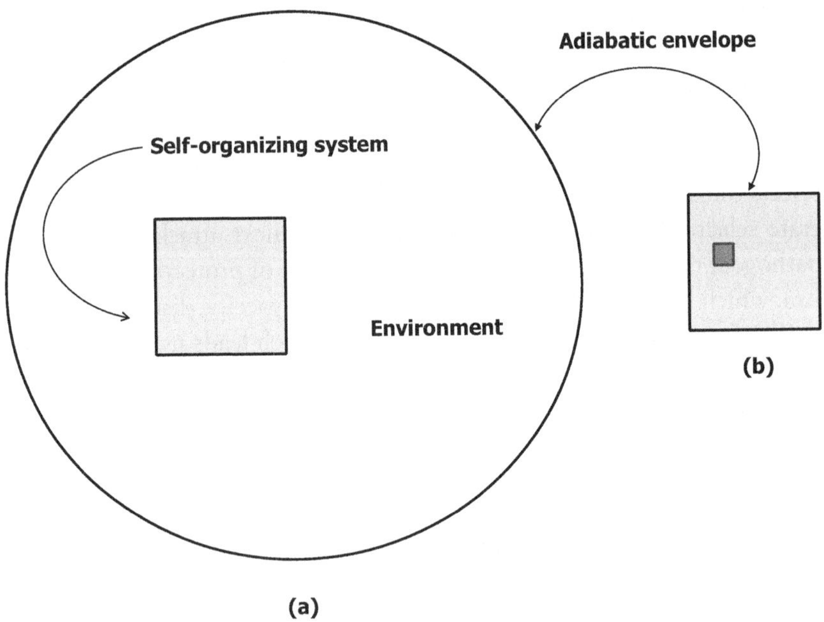

Fig. 4.6 A self-organizing system. (Source: Von Foerster (2003, p. 2))

> universe into two mutually exclusive parts: the one part is completely occupied with a self-organizing system S_0, while the other part we may call the environment E_0 of this organizing system: S_0 & E_0 = U_0 ... Undoubtedly, if this self-organizing system is permitted to do its job of organizing itself for a little while, its entropy must have decreased during this time... In order to accomplish this, the entropy in the remaining part of our finite universe, i.e. the entropy in the environment must have increased ... otherwise the Second Law of Thermodynamics is violated. If now some of the processes which contributed to the decrease of the entropy of the system are irreversible you will find the entropy of the universe U_0 at a higher level than before our system started to organize itself, hence the state of the universe will be more disorganized than before ... in other words, the activity of the system was a disorganizing one, and we may justly call such a system a "disorganizing system"... In spite of this suggested proof of the non-existence of self-organizing systems, I proposed to continue the use of the term "self-organizing system" whilst being aware of the fact that this term becomes meaningless, unless the system is in close contact with an environment, *which possesses available energy and order*, and with which our system is in a state of perpetual interaction, such that it somehow manages to "live" on the expenses of this environment (von Foerster, 2003, pp. 1–3)[3]

The concept of self-organization[4] can be considered a prelude to that of autopoiesis used by Maturana and Varela and by Luhmann.[5] While self-organization refers mainly to how the structures of the system are organized, Maturana—when he was part of the interdisciplinary research group at the University of Illinois at the invitation of von Foerster—highlighted that some systems (he mainly studied the activities of the nervous system) not only internally organize the relationship between the parts but also generate their reproduction, constantly referring to themselves.

[3] The source cited contains an adaptation of the address given at the Interdisciplinary Symposium on Self-Organizing Systems, on May 5, 1959, in Chicago, Illinois.

[4] It is interesting to recall that the term self-organization was used for the first time by Kant, precisely in referring to organisms in which the parts produce each other, anticipating the most advanced systemic conceptions (Capra, 1997, pp. 21–22).

[5] The passage identified (self-regulatory systems/self-organizing systems/autopoietic systems) cannot be framed in a rigid conceptual sequence, since they are superimposed and interrelated models, which are separated only for the purpose of facilitating exposure.

In the subsequent collaboration with Francisco Varela, the term "autopoiesis" was coined to describe the process of a system produced starting from itself, or rather, in which the only product of its organization is the system itself, and thus, there is no separation between producer and product (Maturana & Varela, 1987, pp. 48–49).

The relationship between system and environment, in this perspective, changes radically compared to what is assumed in the theory of open systems. First, autopoietic systems are organizationally closed, in that they maintain their identity by referring to themselves, albeit not being isolated, from an energetic perspective with respect to the outside. Furthermore, the system and its environment coevolve and are co-determined in "structural coupling,"[6] preserving operational closure and organizational autonomy.

This path leads to the description of autopoiesis applied to social systems, the basis of Niklas Luhmann's work and thought, more widely taken up in Sect. 4.3.

As a result of the most recent advances in systemic theories, the contrast between the view of the firm as closed system or as open system is overcome (Vicari, 2024, p. 141). Piaget (1970, 1971) has the merit of having been the first to identify the simultaneous possibility of closure and opening in systems. The closure refers to the constitutive organization of the system (which makes it possible to keep its identity distinct) and to self-reference as an irreplaceable reproduction mechanism. Openness is attributed to the system's ability to draw energetic nourishment from the environment, increasing its complexity.

The simultaneous existence of these features has led to a renewed vision of the system's relationship with the environment and as a consequence can also inspire a different logic of the relationship between the company, understood as a social system, and the meso and macro aggregates to which it relates (environmental context). In fact, the theory of complex systems presents itself today as a theory of the development and evolution of systems capable of existing in unstable, evolutionary, and chaotic environments and of being, in turn, the protagonists of the evolution of the environments in which they themselves operate (Rullani & Vicari, 1999, p. 6).

---

[6] We will return to the concept of "structural coupling" in the next chapter.

4.2 The Use of the Systemic Perspective in Management Studies

Having broadly outlined how our interpretative proposal is placed within the context of the evolution of systemic thought, it is perhaps also worth specifying how it is placed within the framework of the recourse that Management has made to systemic theories.

The use of a systemic perspective in management studies is not without precedent. Many authors have adopted—explicitly or implicitly—a vision of business organizations as systems, in many cases also to analyze the relationship of the company with the surrounding environment. Even so, as already mentioned, the reference to systemic thinking does not identify a single theoretical field as many different points of view are currently framed within it. Furthermore, the omission of precise placement of the various conceptualizations within one system approach rather than within another can generate some confusion. It is useful to make some references to clarify how our interpretation compares with the previous systemic viewpoints used in management studies.

In general, we can establish that, with varying intensity and diffusion, nearly all systemic approaches have been used in management and business organization studies.

Systemic analysis as a methodology in the business field was extremely widespread in the 1960s and the 1970s, with the progressive complexity of industrial production and company organization. Systems-oriented management (Capra, 1997, p. 76) has been widely used, and numerous theoretical formulations have used a systemic concept based on engineering, mathematical, or computer models. The modeling of the enterprise as a cybernetic system, as devised by Stafford Beer (1995), constitutes a stimulating representation of it.

The theory of open systems has also been widely used in business studies. It is implicit in the approach that links contingencies to environmental variables (Galbraith, 1973, 1977; Lawrence & Lorsch, 1967) and in many organizational studies (see, among others, Emery & Trist, 1960; Katz & Kahn, 1966). In particular, once the idea that the company is a system open to the environment had gained traction, a large amount of research shifted attention from the internal operating mechanisms of the company to the social and managerial implications of the relationship with the environment.

Attempts to create a business theory based on the assumptions of the theories on autopoietic systems are rarer (a significant contribution is contained in Vicari, 2024), and the few attempts made in this sense have led to moments of dissent and criticism.

Thus, within the prospect of management studies' recurrent use was made to open systems theories and to the basic holistic approach to systemic thinking, which was then interpreted by resorting, more or less strongly, to a technical systematization of an engineering and mathematical nature. Conversely, fewer attempts have been made to reconnect business phenomena to an interpretation that can be framed in what is defined as the theory of autopoietic systems.

Therefore, responding to the instance contained in the introductory part of this section, we can, at this stage, clarify with greater precision that the interpretative proposal presented hereinafter tends to move away from a vision of the business–environment relationship, such as that recalled by the theory of open systems. From there, it tends to integrate confidently into the line of studies that links systemic identity and its function of being to the degree of complexity found in the surrounding environment and to the needs of systemic selection related to this complexity.

As mentioned, the emphasis put on the precise placement of this writing within the context of systemic thought responds to the fundamental methodological solicitation not to refer generically to the theory of systems but rather to a precise evolutionary moment of this branch of studies. As anticipated, the proposed reading of the company–task environment relationship is, in many ways, linked to the Luhmannian systemic view. Therefore, the next paragraph will briefly clarify some conceptual pillars of Luhmannian theory that will be used in the subsequent interpretation of the firm–environmental context relationship.

4.3 Basic Concepts of Luhmannian Theory on Complex Social Systems

Luhmann's theory of social systems[7] almost always relates coherently to the theory of autopoietic systems developed in Biology by Maturana and Varela (1980), to the theory of self-organizing systems developed in the cybernetics field mainly thanks to the work of von Foerster (see, among others, 2003), and to the new methodological approaches based on complexity, among which Morin's systematization stands out (see, among others, 1977, 2007; Morin et al., 1984).

There is a strongly homogeneous epistemological instance in the stimuli that have influenced these scholars, who—each in their disciplines—have felt the need to move toward new paradigms. In particular, it is interesting to highlight Luhmann's contact, on the one hand, with von Foerster's cybernetic thinking, and on the other hand, with the theories on autopoietic systems developed by Maturana and Varela. In the German sociologist's work, the cybernetics culture has strengthened the orientation toward a systemic anti-subjectivist conceptualization that does not presuppose some individual or collective subject with ordering functions (Febbrajo, 1990, p. 15) while the encounter with the autopoietic theories of Maturana and Varela led to a review of some aspects of his original thought. Indeed, it is possible to distinguish between a first and a second Luhmann, with the adherence to the systemic approach of the two Chilean biologists as a turning point. In the works before 1980, complexity, the central element of all his theoretical approaches, was mainly reported outside the system (leading to an incessant attempt by the system to adapt its internal complexity to this exogenous complexity and to reduce and/or dominate it). In the works of the 1980s (and in particular in Soziale Systeme), the center of gravity shifts within a system oriented toward not only the complexity of the environment but above all to its complexity (Febbrajo, 1990, pp. 16–21). As mentioned, in this passage,

[7] Luhmann's works, from which we drew inspiration, are mainly Luhmann (1969, 1990, 1995, 2016).

we can recognize the fundamental role played by the detailed study of Maturana and Varela's autopoietic approach and the importation of this concept, originally launched in the biological field, into the sociological habitat.

We chose to use a systemic approach developed in a sociological environment in this text as the basis of reference. The particular development of the theory within the social field will allow a more natural recovery of the systemic conceptualizations for the interpretation of the business–environmental context relationship as companies (but also networks, districts, sectors, and markets) are social configurations, the features of which correspond in many ways to those of the systems studied by Luhmann. The latter, moreover, was strongly influenced by the theories of organization, which, along with the German philosophical tradition and legal culture, represent one of the cultural matrixes constantly present in his works (Febbrajo, 1990, pp. 16–17). Luhmann's work demonstrates, in fact, a sensitivity toward the organizational approach (there are also numerous bibliographical references to this line of studies in his work), which, to some extent, simplifies the possibilities of the relevance of his approach with recurring issues in management studies.

Nevertheless, we should not imagine that the traceability of the Luhmannian approach to companies is immediate as the German sociologist is strongly inclined to use complex language and a methodology based on scientific abstraction.[8] In this regard, as will be seen in the following chapters, the use of Luhmann's theory of social systems[9] for the study of micro, meso, and macro relations from the point of view of management studies will converge in an autonomous interpretative framework that uses conceptualizations from other authors as well.

However, for a better understanding of this interpretative framework, it appears essential to share some key concepts of Luhmann's theory on social systems, to which we dedicate the rest of this section.

[8] Abstraction, as a scientific methodology, is strongly present in Luhmann and undoubtedly makes it difficult to read and not always immediate to understand. He consciously uses this approach, considering it an epistemological necessity (Luhmann, 1995, p. li).

[9] It should be clarified that Luhmann's work covers very broad topics and that only the aspects that are most immediately referable to the topic of interest have been examined here.

4.3.1 Complexity

As mentioned, the concept of complexity can be outlined both outside the system (the complexity is in the environment) and inside it (the complexity is in the system). However, as we shall see, these are two intrinsically connected forms of complexity.

External complexity is the excess of the possibilities of experience and action of the world with respect to the system, which, in an attempt to face this complexity (without ever completely succeeding), tries either to increase its experience and action capacity or to reduce the complexity of the environment to make it bearable:

> The term *complexity* is meant to indicate that there are always more possibilities of experience and action that can be actualized. (Luhmann, 1990, p. 26)

From this point of view, complexity gives a reason to the system and makes the system functional for a purpose. The aim is to structure itself to face the difference in complexity between itself and the environment. Nevertheless, the process is endless, insomuch as the continuous enhancement of the system makes it increasingly suitable to capture external complexity. Moreover, the growth of awareness and the improved capacity for perception lead it to become increasingly complex in a circle that feeds itself infinitely.

The shift of complexity within the system entails a change in the viewing angle. The system is no longer oriented only to the complexity existing outside it; rather, it is oriented toward its own complexity as a constitutive element of its own identity. The very structure of the system not only has the objective of facing a complex external environment but also transforms, from the inside, "unstructured complexity into structured complexity" (Luhmann, 1995, p. 282). Such structuring does not require the invariance of the elements that constitute the system and on the contrary, allows one to be able to tolerate any replacements of the elements without changing the identity of the system. In other words, complex systemic structures continue to exist even in the presence of a change in the elements that compose them. The organizational structure of the system guarantees the reproduction of "elements that therefore always appear within existing structural categories yet still always appear as new" (Luhmann, 1995, p. 282). The system's self-reproduction and its own identity are made possible by the selective mechanisms that characterize it rather than by the invariance of the elements that constitute it. This fundamental assumption of Luhmannian thought will be clearer shortly once we have dealt with the concepts of systemic selection and self-reference.

Finally, it should be stressed that by including an internal dimension of the system in the concept of complexity, the idea that the system must above all adapt to the environment is changed (in business theory, this concept has often translated in an attempt to study the environment and to optimize the potential of the firm for adaptation to it). When dealing with systems, there is not only a problem of adaptation to the outside but also one of self-adaptation to their complexity:

> Complex systems must adapt not only to their environments but also to their own complexity. They must cope with internal improbabilities and inadequacies. They must develop mechanisms that build precisely on those failings, such as mechanisms that reduce deviant behavior, behavior that becomes possible only when there are dominant basic structures. (Luhmann, 1995, p. 31)

4.3.2 Difference Between System and Environment

The system is identified by the difference with respect to the environment. The system is constituted thus through the generation and maintenance of a difference with respect to the environment. Each system leaves only itself out of the environment, which, therefore, is defined (and finds unity) negatively with respect to the system. The boundaries of the system regulate the difference between the system and the environment, and the maintenance of these boundaries coincides with the conservation of the system. The environment, on the other hand, is not a system, it has no boundaries, and it is "delimited by open horizons" (Luhmann, 1995, p. 17).

It follows that the difference between system and environment cannot be represented through an absolute division between two complementary entities, as the distinction is a function of each system. Each system defines its environment as that which is other with respect to itself. Each system is part of the environment of all other systems, and the system–environment difference can only be identified for a specific system.

> Everything that happens belongs to a *system* (or to many systems) and *always at the same time* to the *environment of other systems* ... Every change in a system is a change in the environment of other systems; every increase in complexity in one place increases the complexity of the environment for all other systems. (Luhmann, 1995, p. 177)

We have already mentioned that the system–environment dissimilarity presupposes a difference in complexity as no system has "the requisite variety"[10] capable of putting it on the same level of complexity as the environment. Therefore, the location of this difference in complexity also defines the identity of the system as opposed to everything else (Luhmann, 1995, pp. 181–184).

4.3.3 Systemic Selection

Systems act as selective reducers, selecting the pulses coming from outside and concurrently transforming the external complexity into internal complexity (Fig. 4.7).

As mentioned, the system lacks the requisite variety to address the difference in complexity with respect to the environment. The latter has a higher degree of complexity when compared with the system. If the system had a complexity equal to that of the environment, it would no longer have reason to exist, insomuch as it is defined as being different from its environment precisely because of this difference in complexity. The system compensates for the inferiority in terms of complexity with a capacity for systemic selection of its structure. In other words, "a system can become complex only by selecting an order" (Luhmann, 1995, p. 26).

[10] See Sect. 1.4.1, Chap. 1.

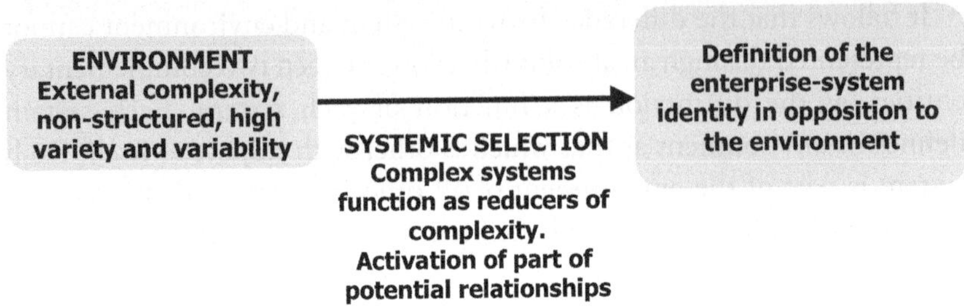

Fig. 4.7 System–environment relationship: Systemic selection

The selection also acts within the system. The greater the number of elements a system must keep in connection within its interior and to which it must relate in its reference environment, the more difficult it becomes to correlate each element to the others. A complex system is precisely a system in which it is impossible to connect each element with all the others. Given that, as the number of elements increases arithmetically, the possible relationships between them grow in geometric progression. Complex systems activate only a part of the potential relationships, selectively connecting the elements (Luhmann, 1995, pp. 24–25). From an internal structural point of view, the system carries out a selection among multiple combinatorial possibilities and selectively establishes relationships between the elements. This selection remains constant and gives identity to the system even in the event of a substitution of the single elements. In this sense, a system gives life to an organized complexity, that is, to a complexity endowed with selective relationships between the elements (Luhmann, 1995, pp. 24–25).

Hence, since complexity produces an excess of possibilities when compared with those that are accessible, the system continuously selects and internally self-selects some relationships among the many that can be achieved.

The systemic selection defines an option for the system: a relationship becomes a reality in the face of an infinite number of possible relationships that remain nonactivated.[11] This concept is linked, in Luhmannian theory, to that of contingency, that is, the creation of a form (not necessarily the best one) in the presence of far more numerous potentials.

[11] In this sense, the enterprise-system does not submit passively to the influences of the environment; rather, it selects the environmental stimuli through the formation of action schemes (Vicari, 2024, pp. 156–158).

Everything that is not chosen remains latent, potentially available (Luhmann, 1995, p. 337):

> The term *contingency* is intended to express the fact that the possibilities of further experience and action indicated in the horizon of actual experience are just that—possibilities—and might turn out differently than expected. (Luhmann, 1990, p. 26)

The continuous choice of some of the relationships among the many possible ones also explains why very different systems can be generated from similar units (Luhmann, 1995, p. 25). The continuous selection process in connecting the elements affects the system by configuring it uniquely.

Complexity imposes a choice, yet such a choice is guaranteed by high degrees of freedom as the selection process can be addressed differently. One of the most important features of Luhmannian thought is, indeed, the constant awareness that next to the concrete world of the so-called social reality, there is an invisible world and therefore one that is only imaginable but very important for understanding the preceding world: the world of that which is possible. Reality does not have as its opposite the world of unreality, scientifically relevant only to be eliminated and excluded. It is instead opposed to a different reality, not a current one, but, in fact, a possible one (Febbrajo, 1990, pp. 47–48), with which the system could maintain a potential exchange through a change in the selection processes.

An important passage connected with the theme of systemic selection is that on the conception of time (Luhmann, 1995, pp. 41–43). Time acts on the link between complexity and selection. The exploitation of time makes it possible to multiply the possible relationships by placing them in succession. In this sense, time becomes an extension of choice. Theoretically, if the time reference could be expanded to infinity, the selection would have no meaning in complex systems as the elements could be made interdependent with one another (Luhmann, 1995, p. 42). As the time available is not infinite, the use of it by the system does not eliminate the need for selection; however, it manages to increase the possibilities allowed in the system, partially transforming the exclusions into references.

4.3.4 Self-Reference

Self-reference constitutes, in contemporary systems theory, an advanced moment of rethinking regarding tradition. As already mentioned, the evolution of systemic thought has not led to the rejection or denial of its conceptual bases but rather to a progressive enrichment of them. One of these rethinking passages can be linked to the introduction of the concept of the system's self-reference. An autopoietic system is not only capable of self-representing itself and of having a description of itself (through a capacity for self-observation and self-knowledge) as differentiated from the rest (and, therefore, regarding its environment), but it is also capable of reproducing this difference. Self-referential systems "have the ability to establish relations with themselves and to differentiate these relations with their environment" (Luhmann, 1995, p. 13), and self-reference "is an operation by which the system indicates itself in contrast to its environment" (Luhmann, 1995, p. 444).

The concept of self-reference implies that the system, in activating (selective) relationships among the elements, continually refers to its survival, making it possible to perpetuate self-reproduction. In this sense, autopoietic systems are called closed systems as they are self-sufficient in the mechanisms that sanction their reproduction and as these processes can only be used within the system itself. In this passage, the importation into the social sphere of autopoietic theory referred to by Maturana and Varela to living systems is evident.

This does not mean that autopoietic systems do not have environmental sensitivity, that they do not exchange energy with the outside, or that they are isolated. Rather, it means that they are self-referential in generating the conditions for their reproduction, allowing their identity to be protected over time. This results in a reversal in the conditions for adapting the system to the environment (or of a company to the context[12]) compared with those hypothesized by the theorists of open systems. An input–output model was in force for the latter, in which adaptation was defined as a response of the system to environmental concerns. In the

[12] For a dissertation on the concept of self-reference applied to the firm, see Vicari (2024, pp. 29–32).

systemic concept based on self-reference, instead, the relationship with the outside is selected according to the processes of self-reproduction within the system.

4.3.5 Meaning

The concepts we have focused on thus far can be related to a basic notion in Luhmann's theory, namely, that of meaning.

Meaning is the strategy that guides selection in conditions of high complexity (Luhmann, 1969, p. 257). The selection made on the basis of meaning involves the actualization of one of the infinite opportunities offered to the system and presents the chance of continuous reference to other possibilities of action (Fig. 4.8).

A selection made on the basis of meaning implies the current denial of other possibilities, which, however, are not permanently eliminated but remain latent:

> The phenomenon of meaning appears as a surplus of references to other possibilities of experience and action. Something stands in the focal point, at the center of the intention, and all else is indicated marginally as the horizon of an "and so forth" of experience and action…The totality of the references presented by a meaningfully intended object offers more to hand

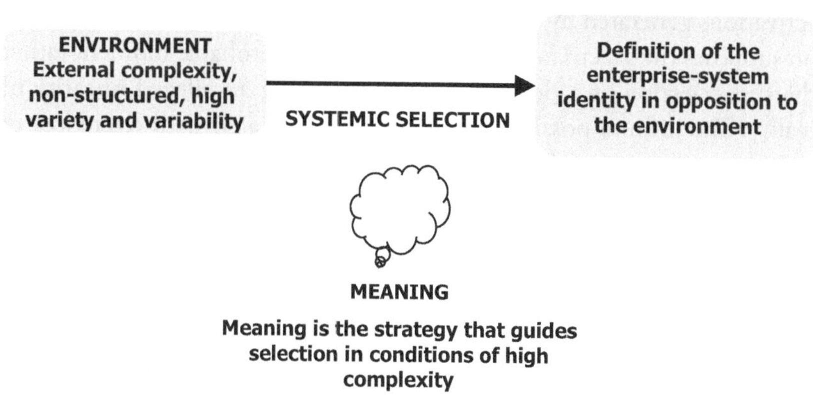

Fig. 4.8 System–environment relationship: Meaning

> that can in fact be actualized at any moment. Thus the form of meaning, through its referential structure, *forces* the next step, to *selection*. (Luhmann, 1995, p. 60)

The possibilities of references are potentially endless and can be reached through a series of selective actions carried out by the system. The world of that which is possible remains at all times potentially accessible, generating an exuberance of possibilities for action:

> In a somewhat different formulation, one could say that meaning equips an actual experience or action with redundant possibilities. Thereby the uncertainty of the selection is offset once again. Redundancy serves the function of a guarantee. One can afford mistakes, because all possibilities are not yet exhausted. One can return to the starting point and choose another path. (Luhmann, 1995, p. 60)

The information available to the system can reduce complexity by addressing the selection and limiting the possibilities of choice. In any case, the references activated by meaning always give the possibility of making new references just as they imply the opportunity to generate different and even contradictory conditions with respect to the current ones. In every selection, the circumstance that it could also be otherwise is implicit, which makes the current condition contingent.

It is important to underline the potentially contradictory nature of the activations generated by meaning. As mentioned, the logic of complexity presupposes the acceptance of contradiction as a probable moment rather than its rejection as a deviant element regarding an alleged linearity of reality. The infinite possibilities that can be activated with references of meaning presuppose the possibility of reference even to inconsistent forms. This leaves the system in a perennial state of alarm, destroying the system's claim to be a complexity already reduced and orderly:

> For an instant, then, indeterminate complexity is restored, and everything is possible. *But at the same time, contradictions possess enough form to guarantee the connectivity of communicative process via meaning.* The system's reproduction is merely directed into different paths. Forms of meaning appear to be inconsistent, and this causes alarm. But the system's *autopoiesis*

> is *not interrupted*. It goes on. The honor of being the first to have formulated this goes to Hegel's conception of "dialectic." (Luhmann, 1995, p. 373)

Meaning closes the circuit that links the concepts of complexity, difference system–environment, systemic selection, and self-reference. Complexity imposes a selection guided by the meaning, which, far from defining a path of linear sequences, opens up endless alternatives at all times, even in contradiction with the actuality of the system. However, as long as the system manages to maintain self-reference, even deviating on different and contradictory paths, it continues to generate its self-reproduction, selectively actualizing one of the many possibilities offered. The system ends only if it loses reference to itself.

4.3.6 Systemic Differentiation

A process of differentiation within the system also exists. The differentiations that occur within the system (systemic differentiation) take place within the systemic boundary and therefore in a protected environment, where there is already a partial reduction of the complexity:

> System differentiation is nothing more than the repetition of system formation within systems. Further system/environment differences can be differentiated within systems. The entire system then acquires the function of an "internal environment" for these subsystems, indeed, for each subsystem in its own specific way. The system/environment difference is therefore duplicated; the entire system multiplies itself as a multiplicity of system/environment differences ... Therefore system differentiation is a process of increasing complexity that greatly affects what can be observed as the unity of the entire system. (Luhmann, 1995, p. 18)

The same process of distinction between system and environment we had observed for the global system is reproduced internally, between subsystem and subsystem–environment (defined, by difference, as everything else).[13] Internal differentiation, on the one hand, increases the

[13] For a review of this concept with respect to the firm, see Vicari (2024, pp. 127–128).

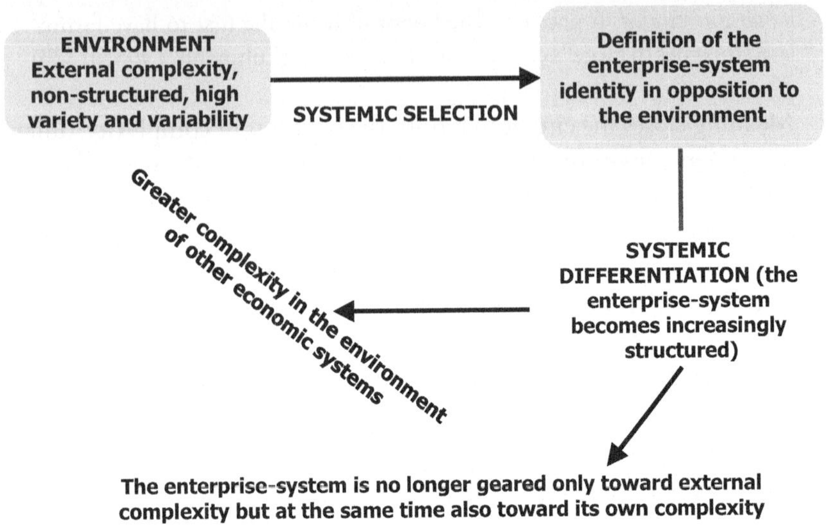

Fig. 4.9 System–environment relationship: Systemic differentiation

internal complexity of the system as it makes the global system more articulated; on the other hand, internal differentiation reduces complexity as the subsystems take on a part of the total complexity.

Accordingly, as shown in Fig. 4.9, the system differentiates itself regarding the environment through a systemic selection guided by meaning, and in an attempt to deal with the excess of external complexity, it differentiates internally into subsystems (systemic differentiation) with two important consequences:

- The system becomes increasingly structured and is no longer only oriented toward managing the external complexity but also its internal complexity.
- The system, by organizing itself internally, introduces new complexity into the environment of other systems.

In giving an example of the company and the phenomenon of the growing digitalization of economic systems, we could say that the company resorts to digitalization to cope with external complexity. Digitalization allows it to process the data it needs more quickly and effectively (information on consumers, suppliers, competitors, and so on) and optimize its processes of producing goods and delivering services. To complete this digitalization, however, the company needs to increase its internal complexity (create new divisions, acquire and maintain suitable machinery and software, nourish the digital skills of its human resources, learn to read the outputs of artificial intelligence, etc.). The consequences are, on the one hand, becoming more complex internally and turning its attention also toward this internal complexity; on the other hand, inducing other companies and other economic systems operating in the environment to adapt to this new digital standard, thereby making the environment of the companies and the economic actors more complex.

4.3.7 Interpenetration

The delicate issue of the relationship between human being and social systems (also recurring in management studies) is addressed by Luhmann using the concept of interpenetration. According to the humanistic tradition, the individual was placed within the social system while the Luhmannian approach suggests changing this assumption, considering human being external to the social system as part of the environment. The individual, external to the social system and part of its environment, is, in turn, a system, in respect of which the observed social system is placed within his/her environment:

> If one views human beings as part of the environment of society (instead of as part of society itself), this changes the premises of all the traditional questions, including those of classical humanism. It does not mean that the human being is estimated as less important than traditionally. Anyone who thinks so (and such an understanding either explicitly or implicitly underlies all polemics against this proposal) has not understood the paradigm change in systems theory. (Luhmann, 1995, p. 212)

If we accept these assumptions—that is, that the social system and the individual are two systems, one being part of the environment of the other—we can configure the relationship between the two as a relationship of interpenetration. Interpenetration describes a relationship between systems—each belonging to the other's environment—that makes them reciprocally available, introducing their complexity into the other.

In any case, interpenetrating systems remain independent and constitute their uniqueness on the basis of the selection they individually implement in creating relationships between the elements, a selection that guarantees their distinct autopoiesis. Luhmann is wary of depicting interpenetration with spatial metaphors, such as that of two intersecting circles. Interpenetration presupposes at the same time inclusion, as interpenetrating systems also use the complexity coming from the other system, and exclusion, as two distinct mechanisms of autopoiesis must exist to speak of interpenetration (Luhmann, 1995, pp. 217–221).

However, the interpenetration relationship is constitutive for the systems that participate in it. It presupposes mutual participation in the formation of the elements and events belonging to each other. The relationship generated as a result of interpenetration, therefore, is not a simple sharing of systemic spaces, nor does it consist solely of the provision of reciprocal inputs of energy and information. Interpenetration goes further, assuming the mutual availability of the systems in question to participate in the formation of each other (Luhmann, 1995, pp. 217–218) and therefore to generate their autopoietic processes (which remain distinct) using a portion of the complexity of the other as well.

In this sense, social systems do not include individuals, but rather, it represents them as autonomous, despite participating in the constitution of the system. This approach, far from diminishing the importance of the individual, strengthens it, admitting that the human being cannot be reduced to a simple element of a system but that he/she is the bearer of his/her autonomous complexity. Such complexity is not limited to any specific social system; it is made available to different social systems (business, family, religious community, etc.) through a multiplicity of interpenetrating relationships.

There is, therefore, a fundamental difference between systemic *differentiation*, which presupposes an articulation of the subsystem–environment differences within the original system, and interpenetration, in which the two interpenetrating systems remain in the environment of each other while making their complexity available for the construction of another system.

References

Ashby, W. R. (1962). Principles of the Self-Organizing System. In H. von Foerster & G. W. Zopf Jr. (Eds.), *Principles of Self-Organization: Transactions of the University of Illinois Symposium*. Pergamon Press.

Beer, S. (1995). *Brain of the Firm. The Managerial Cybernetics of Organization* (2nd ed.). John Wiley & Sons.

Capra, F. (1997). *The Web of Life. A New Synthesis of Mind and Matter*. HarperCollins Publishers.

Emery, F. E., & Trist, E. L. (1960). Socio-Technical Systems. In C. W. Churchman & M. Verhulst (Eds.), *Management Science, Models and Techniques* (Vol. 2). Pergamon Press.

Febbrajo, A. (1990). Introduzione all'edizione italiana. In N. Luhmann, *Sistemi sociali. Fondamenti di una teoria generale*. Il Mulino.

Galbraith, J. R. (1973). *Designing Complex Organizations*. Addison-Wesley.

Galbraith, J. R. (1977). *Organization Design*. Addison-Wesley.

Katz, D., & Kahn, R. L. (1966). *Social Psychology of Organization*. John Wiley & Sons.

Lawrence, P. R., & Lorsch, J. W. (1967). *Organization and Environment: Managing Differentiation and Integration*. Harvard University Press.

Luhmann, N. (1969). Moderne Systemtheorien als Form gesamtgesellschaftlicher Analyse. In T. W. Adorno (Ed.), *Spätkapitalismus oder Industriegesellschaft?: Verhandlungen des 16 Deutschen Soziologentages*. Enke.

Luhmann, N. (1990). *Essays on Self-Reference*. Columbia University Press.

Luhmann, N. (1995). *Social Systems*. Standford University Press.

Luhmann, N. (2016). *Gesellschaftsstruktur und Semantik. Studien zur Wissenssoziologie der modernen Gesellschaft. Band 2*. Suhrkamp.

Maturana, H. R., & Varela, F. J. (1980). *Autopoiesis and Cognition. The Realization of Living*. D. Reidel Publishing Company.

Maturana, H. R., & Varela, F. J. (1987). *The Tree of Knowledge. The Biological Roots of Human Understanding*. Shambhala Publications.

Morin, E. (1977). *La Méthode. I. La Nature de la nature*. Editions Seuil.

Morin, E. (2007). Le vie della complessità. In G. Bocchi & M. Ceruti (Eds.), *La sfida della complessità*. Bruno Mondadori Editori.

Morin, E., Atias, C., & Le Moigne, J. L. (Eds.). (1984). *Science et Conscience de la Complexité. Echenges avec Edgar Morin*. Libraire de l'Université.

Piaget, J. (1970). *L'epistémologie génétique*. Presses universitaires de France.

Piaget, J. (1971). *Biology and Knowledge: An Essay on the Relations between Organic Regulations and Cognitive Processes*. University of Chicago Press.

Rullani, E., & Vicari, S. (1999). Introduzione. In E. Rullani & S. Vicari (Eds.), (1999) *Sistemi ed evoluzioni nel management*. Etas.

Varela, J. V. (2007). Complessità del cervello e autonomia del vivente. In G. Bocchi & M. Ceruti (Eds.), *La sfida della complessità*. Bruno Mondadori Editori.

Vicari, S. (2024). *The Living Firm. Journey into a Different Conception*. Amazon Publishing.

von Bertalanffy, L. (1969). *General System Theory: Foundations, Development, Applications*. G. Braziller.

von Foerster, H. (2003). On Self-Organizing Systems and Their Environments. In H. von Foerster (Ed.), *Understanding Understanding. Essays on Cybernetics and Cognition*. Springer Verlag.

5

A Possible Reinterpretation of the Micro, Meso, and Macro Relationships in the Context of Complexity

Abstract In this chapter we evaluate—for the purposes of studying the micro, meso, and macro relationships in the *Economics of Complexity*—the potential of using an approach that is close to the logic of complex social systems.

If we represent the company as a self-referential system, we admit that it is primarily interested in self-reproducing the conditions of its existence. It defines itself as a system for tackling the complexity of the environment and aims to continuously regenerate its diversity with respect to the surrounding world; for this purpose, the enterprise system implements a "systemic selection," based on its "meaning," which continuously refers to this reproduction. The organization of the company as a system also implies that any success achieved by it, in terms of stability or reproduction, makes the environment of all other systems more complex. Thus, it follows that whenever an entrepreneurial form is capable of overcoming its challenge with the complexity of the reference context even temporarily, it brings about not only new complexity within it but also renewed complexity in its reference environment. The enterprise system, in fact, is in turn part of the environment of other systems—among

C. Mazzoni, *Firms, Industries, Markets*, https://doi.org/10.1007/978-3-031-59823-4_5

which we can identify other companies (competitors, suppliers, customers, and partners) and broader systems (sectors or markets)—and any increase in complexity within it produces an increase in complexity in the environment of these other systems.

Keywords Company task environment relations in the complex systems' theoretical perspective • The redefinition of objects of study from the perspective of self-referential systems • The boundaries between system and environment as stabilizers of differences in complexity • The systemic selection of possible relationships: The role of structure and concept of an enacted environment • A methodological issue: The choice of the observation point and construction of causal connections

5.1 Company–Task Environment Relations in the Complex Systems' Theoretical Perspective

Having clarified, even if briefly, some of the concepts that will be used below, we can now return to the core of our discussion (the relationship between the company and task environment in the *Economics of Complexity*) with a renewed wealth of cognitive tools.

We have seen how, together with the progressive complication of phenomenical reality, the interpretation of phenomena has also become more sophisticated.[1] We observed in Chap. 3, in this regard, how all the theoretical perspectives used in economic studies (the mechanical–aggregative, causal–structuralist, and strategic–competitive point of view) have deviated over time to some extent toward attempts to represent complexity.

Important interpretative proposals are suggested by these deviations. The inclusion of uncertainty and experimentation in decision-making processes (from Simon's thought to the theory of games), the Porterian

[1] It is worth recalling here too that epistemological complexity is not only a consequence of increased phenomenological complexity but also contributes, in turn, to generating complexity in reality as it attributes the dignity of analysis to previously rarely studied phenomena (see Sect. 1.4, Chap. 1).

reinterpretation of the structuralist system, Yip's revolutionary thesis on "gateways to entry," the Abellian intuition of a mobile business based on the change of the actors' competitive scheme and the advances of the strategic studies (emphasis on emerging strategies and dynamic capabilities, configuration of the company as a network of relationships, legitimization of sets—networks, districts, populations, strategic groups—as a unit of analysis) have represented significant steps in the path of the theory of the firm (and, in particular, in the line of studies that deals with studying the company in relation to its task environment) toward the logic of complexity.

Many of the approaches identified as turning points have to some extent improved the representation of complexity in the relationships that are generated between the micro object of our study (the company) and the meso and macro context of reference (industries and markets). The objective was achieved either by heavily sophisticating the analysis methodologies (e.g., the mathematical structures that support multi-variable interaction models in the theory of games) or, *vice versa*, by making the models to be used conceptually very flexible (this is what happens, e.g., in Abell's three-dimensional construction that, based on the representation of business by the competitors, has the merit of representing the task environment in a consistently variable manner).

Continuing along this interpretative path, we now evaluate—for the purposes of studying the micro, meso, and macro relationships in the *Economics of Complexity*—the potential of using an approach that is close to the logic of complex social systems. On this point, a premise should be reiterated. The priority reference to the logic of complex social systems in this work is placed within a vision that, in certain cases, deviates from the original approach of the Luhmannian work, drawing on conceptual contributions from other authors as well, in a recomposition that presents elements of novelty and autonomy.

The complex systems' theoretical perspective enables us to examine the relationship not by adapting to the complexity but by starting from it, elevating it to a priority object of study while incorporating it transversally throughout the entire path that crosses the research themes.

If we represent the company as a self-referential system, we admit that it is primarily interested in self-reproducing the conditions of its existence.

It defines itself as a system for tackling the complexity of the environment and aims to continuously regenerate its diversity with respect to the surrounding world; for this purpose, it implements a systemic selection, based on its meaning, which continuously refers to this reproduction. The attempt to address the redundancy of experience and action existing in the external world pushes the enterprise-system to create a structure within itself, which gives rise to a selective reduction of the relationships activated with respect to the multiplicity of possible relationships.

Nowadays, apparently, a part of this reduction in complexity takes place through big data and Artificial Intelligence that allow the company to study the needs of individual consumers and to reach them through one-to-one communication. In hyper-segmentation, the tools of digital transformation generate the illusion of a potential domination by the enterprise-system over the complexity of consumer markets. However, as previously noted in Sect. 4.3.6, Chap. 4, digitalization implies a greater complexity of the internal structure of the enterprise-system (in terms of skills, machinery, and software), orienting it toward its own complexity over time.

The organization of the company as a system also implies that any success achieved by it, in terms of stability or reproduction, makes the environment of all other systems more complex (it is an adaptation to the company, of what Luhmann (1995, p. 182) claims. Thus, it follows that whenever an entrepreneurial form is capable of overcoming its challenge with the complexity of the reference context even temporarily, it brings about not only new complexity within it but also renewed complexity in its reference environment. The enterprise-system, in fact, is in turn part of the environment of other systems—among which we can identify other companies (competitors, suppliers, customers, and partners) and broader systems (sectors or markets)—and any increase in complexity within it produces an increase in complexity in the environment of these other systems. In this sense, referring to the previous example once again, hyper-segmentation action can generate new complexity for suppliers (request for specific raw materials and specific semi-finished products), for distributors (implementation of logistics channels according to the identified needs), for competitors (who will set processes in motion to counteract the company's action), for employees and external staff (who will have to direct their contribution to the realization of finalized services), and so forth.

It is thus precisely the complexity (external and internal) that gives meaning to the company as a system, namely as a structured organization. If there were no differences in complexity, the company would need neither to organize itself as a selective reducer of possible relationships nor to differentiate itself from the surrounding world, becoming a system.

It may be appropriate to continue with a detailed study of this interpretative proposal by reviewing the four scientific research themes addressed in Chap. 2. In that circumstance, it was said that the issues posed by the *Economics of Complexity* in analyzing company–task environment relationships can be grouped into four large, interrelated areas:

- The complexity and consequent opacity of the entities being studied, that is, of the company and the meso- and macroaggregates with which it relates (industries and markets above all).
- The difficulty of identifying boundaries between these entities.
- The unpredictability of the results of the micro, meso, and macro relationships.
- The plurality of possible views on micro, meso, and macro relations and the scientific judgment on these relations.

In Chap. 2, the four research themes were presented in a problematic manner. It is now time to revisit the four themes in the light of a reinterpretation that considers the potential offered by the complex systems' theoretical perspective.

5.2 The Redefinition of Objects of Study from the Perspective of Self-Referential Systems

As previously mentioned, an initial difficulty in the analysis of micro, meso, and macro relationships comes precisely from the complexity and opacity of the objects of study (company, sectors, and markets); complexity and opacity that make them even difficult to identify.

The interpretation of the micro, meso, and macro relationships based on the conceptualization of the company as a complex social system neither shirks the theme of complexity nor attempts to address it as an exogenous aspect. In this approach, complexity is used to arrive at the definition of the objects of our study and to explain their shared evolution. The enterprise-system exists because there is a context from which to differentiate, whereas the latter takes on meaning only as a function of the enterprise itself (Vicari, 2024, p. 153). In fact, the enterprise-system finds its own justification in the objective—never realized—of dominating the complexity of the reference environment, just as the complexity of the latter is accentuated precisely by the presence of the systems, which—to fight complexity—contribute to increasing it. The theory of systems not only avoids, in this sense, any attempt at circumvention with respect to the need to take note of complexity but rather allows all reasoning starting from the inevitability of such evidence.

The approach suggested does not oblige an absolute definition of the company, sector, and markets (we have seen how this universal description is practically impossible nowadays); it rather specifies the objects of study starting from the selected point of view. A point of view that, in theory, can coincide with that of one of the systems that interest us, even if it is concretely affected by the interpretative filter of the observant subject.[2]

By observing the micro, meso, and macro relationships from the perspective of a specific company, we can identify the company as an autopoietic system and, by difference, the environment of that enterprise-system. Therefore, in this case, the company is initially identified as a system and then the environment is recognized as *something else*. The same can be done if the perspective of a different system is considered

[2] This is one of the divergent aspects of the thesis proposed with respect to the original approach theory of social systems by Luhmann, who believes that the choice of the "system" point of view is the only correct one. Although conceptually agreeing with the idea that it is the system and thus the company that defines its own difference from the environment and that it is therefore necessary to reconstruct this perspective of observation, it is quite difficult to fully assume the point of view of the enterprise-system operationally as observers of the company–task environment relationship (researchers, consultants, entrepreneurs, and managers) are often conditioned by their perceptive and interpretative codes, which do not coincide with the systemic ones. We will return to this issue in Sect. 5.5.

(another company, network, district, business area, sector, or market). The reference context is always defined by difference.

The configuration described depends on the system that is related to the analysis and on the perspective of observation of the observer, according to a correct methodology.[3] In a similar light, it is incoherent to establish universally what the sector is, what the market is, or what the company is or where one ends and the others begin. It is not possible, looking back at one of the examples cited in a problematic manner, to define a priori whether, in a network, the system to be studied is the network itself or the individual company participating in the coalition. This definition depends on the system's point of view that, at a given moment, is conceiving the difference between itself and the rest or from the point of view of the observer who, in given circumstances, recognizes a certain unity (or a grouping of units) as a system. For example, a district can be looked at globally, in its dimension as a local productive system, as an autopoietic system, equipped with its own identity and autonomy, related to the outside through a selection process that defines the conditions of its self-reproduction. Similar reasoning can be established for all the hybrid formulas that have been cited as a demonstration of the opacity of the micro, meso, and macro relationships. For example, this applies to supply chains, integrated factories, industrial condominiums, large-scale retail distribution, marketing networks, internal entrepreneurship initiatives, collaborative and competitive spin-offs, and franchising. It is not important to define absolutely the entities that are the object of our study. They will be defined from time to time according to the difference between what the system is and what the environment is, based on a certain point of view.

As has been said, there is an additional difficulty: the company (as well as the other units studied) is an observed object and an observing subject simultaneously. The company is, in fact, a participant in the micro, meso, and macro relationship as not only an object but also a subject that observes and interprets what happens in the surrounding environment. It gives its own representation of events, and its behaviors follow this

[3] We will return to this topic in Sect. 5.5.

interpretation. For example, the enterprise-system observing its environment recognizes different systems in it (i.e., other enterprises or markets) with which it can establish selective relationships:

> Every system must reckon with other systems in its environment. Depending on the depth with which the environment can be perceived, more systems and more different kinds of systems appear in it. (Luhmann, 1995, p. 187)

Obviously, the behavior of the company, a function of its vision, will affect the environment itself and the systems found in it. In this sense, every event will always belong simultaneously to a system and environment of other systems: every change within a system will involve a change in the environment of all other systems, enhancing the reciprocal complexity.

In referring to this initial topic of research—the complexity of the objects of study—we must also consider the phenomena of differentiation within the enterprise-system, which, as we have seen, push to create further system-environment distinctions within the original enterprise-system, generating subsystems that exist within the boundary of the enterprise and absorb a portion of the overall complexity of the system. In this sense, the network or the district can be interpreted as unitary systems, within which there are subsystems capable of producing a system-environment distinction within their boundary.

As a result, the internal differentiation is a way to allow the absorption of variety. It is both an element of additional complexity and an additional factor of evolution. The surpluses and redundancies within the system generate evolutionary potential, while simultaneously producing new limitations, new selections, and renewed complexity. Through the perspective of internal differentiation, we can look at some of the phenomena mentioned above, such as networks, districts, internal entrepreneurship, or integrated factories, wherein we can identify a boundary of the overall system, within which further system-environment distinctions are generated by internal differentiation.

Thus, the systemic rationality linked to complexity presupposes a weakening of the deterministic representation model, assuming we agree on the circumstance that a unique interpretation cannot describe the micro, meso, and macro relationships in the *Economics of Complexity*. The vision taken from the theory of social systems, of a self-referential nature, allows us to have a flexible landmark, capable of implementing changes in state without any force while depicting the objects of the company–task environment relationship according to the point of observation.

5.3 The Boundaries Between System and Environment as Stabilizers of Differences in Complexity

The second scientific research theme, closely related to the first one, is that of identifying boundaries that separate the micro object of economic studies (the company) from its environment. It has been said that in the *Economics of Complexity*, the progressive opacification of traditional references has been accompanied by the loss of a concrete perception of the demarcations between these entities. Therefore, there is an objective difficulty in establishing where the micro dimension ends and where the meso and macro dimensions begin.

In the systemic logic that is being used, the boundaries depend on the realization method of the autopoiesis (Vicari, 2024, p. 141): the activities that allow the reproduction of the system remain within the enterprise-system, whereas the others are external. Companies, as systems, self-generate their boundaries in this sense. Companies know their boundaries because they choose them according to the activities necessary for their self-reproduction, and this choice may vary over time.

Boundaries have an indispensable function because their presence allows the enterprise-system to regulate the difference from its environmental context, thereby defining its own identity. Boundary maintenance, in such a scenario, is identified with the conservation of the system (Luhmann, 1995, p. 17).

The boundaries neither imply an interruption of the connections between the inside and outside nor indicate that the internal relationships are denser than those generated between the company and the reference context. Simply put, the boundary requires that the methods of connection between inside and outside continue in different manners than those that occur within the enterprise-system.

As a result, the boundary can be interpreted as a third component of the relationship, a membrane that stands between the company and the environmental context, stabilizing the difference in level of complexity. It has the dual purpose of not only separating the company from the environment but also generating a link between the two. The company, according to this interpretation, is a closed system as it is self-referential in its reproduction processes; however, at the same time, it is an open system because it has relationships with its reference environment. Thus, although the elements can be part of either the system or the environment at a given moment, relationships can also exist between the company and the environment: the boundary separates the events but enables their causal effects to pass (Luhmann, 1995, pp. 28–29).

This understanding of boundaries can help visualize a demarcation between the company and the environment that is not particularly connected with concretely identifiable parameters on the space–time front (such as the territory, perimeter of the plant, or social community of reference) and to represent "systems which do not come wrapped in a skin" (von Foerster, 2003, p. 6).

In this sense, the complex systems' theoretical perspective provides a key to revisit some interpretative issues raised, for example, regarding the description of the micro, meso, and macro relationships in networks, districts, and cooperation agreements in general. If it is accepted that the company defines itself by difference with respect to its environment (and functionally to the autopoietic process) and if we admit that the boundary does not mark an interruption but only a change in the methods of relationships, it is perhaps possible to interpret the network or the district as systems (internally differentiated) wherein there is a method of internal relationships that clarifies the boundary with respect to what is an environment. This boundary does not interrupt the relations of the network or district with the environment, but it recognizes a different method of continuing the relationship externally. More generally, this applies within initiatives based on cooperative agreements (where the partnership generated because of the coalition can be considered a system), wherein coordination is linked to the existence of rules that regulate relationships between partner companies that are different than those intervening in the market. Moreover, as these entities can be interpreted as the result of a design of internal differentiations (e.g., the individual units that participate in the network, which, as we have mentioned, absorb a portion of complexity locally), the external boundary functions as the skin tissue of the entire system.

These boundaries are susceptible to changes (incremental or decremental) insomuch as they are redefined in response to disturbances for the survival process. Thus, in a company, new units can be received within the system (i.e., through acquisition processes) or new subsystems can be produced through internal differentiation (i.e., through internal entrepreneurship programs), which results in a potential increase in boundary areas. *Vice versa*, expulsions of elements previously internal to the system are possible (e.g., competitive spin-offs or closure of some divisions) that generate, at least theoretically, a decrease in boundary bodies. In each of these circumstances, the boundary remains as a constituent element of the enterprise-system as it stabilizes the relationship with the existing complexity outside it and provides a decoding in the communicative acts with the other systems (belonging to the environment) with which it comes in contact. It is therefore incorrect to speak of a company without borders; a company must have defined borders and the existence of the company only makes sense inasmuch as the system defines what distinguishes itself from a specific environment (Vicari, 2024, p. 140).

In other words, the boundaries can widen or shrink excessively, but they cannot disappear because this circumstance, which prevents the recognizability of the difference between the enterprise-system and its environment, would entail the collapse of the systemic structure and the impossibility of perceiving it as a separate identity with respect to its reference context. The variations in the system's boundaries over time never imply a dissolution of the boundaries. The latter remain in control of the places of external contact, playing a role of transcoding and mediation of the external complexity while reducing internal complexity "with the result that a contact mediated by boundaries cannot convey to any system the full complexity of another" (Luhmann, 1995, p. 29). The boundary protects the enterprise-system and prevents it—encountering other systems—from capturing their total complexity or making its full complexity available to them.

5.4 The Systemic Selection of Possible Relationships: The Role of Structure and Concept of an Enacted Environment

The third of the four scientific research topics concerns the unpredictability of the results of the micro, meso, and macro relationships. The difficulty of prediction stems from the complexity and interdependence of behaviors, from the feedback effects that are generated among "non-trivial machines"—analytically indeterminable, which are dependent on history and therefore unpredictable (von Foerster, 2007, p. 107)—and from the company's difficulty in being both an observed object and an observing subject of the relationship (having to produce an interpretation of the meso- and macroeconomic reality in which it is, itself, a participant). In fact, similar to what happens in physics with Heisenberg's principle,[4] the observation influences the results of the experimentation to a certain extent, making it even more difficult to predict the effects that are generated.

The results of the micro, meso, and macro relationships are determined, at least in part,[5] by the selective activity of the enterprise-system with respect to the limitless possibilities that are created. In fact, the company as a system selects some of the infinite opportunities of relationship and action, by limiting the number of connections actually acted out, internally and externally, to reduce the perceived difference in complexity between the company itself and the external environment. The possibilities that are not pursued and relationships that are not activated are not definitively rejected but remain latent, potentially available for any subsequent paths. As previously mentioned, the enterprise-system carries out a selective reduction guided by meaning. According to Vicari (2024, pp. 162–163), meaning can be assimilated to what, in business theory, has been called leading strategic orientation, which can be adequately expressed as "vision."

[4] See Sect. 1.4.1, Chap. 1.

[5] We will clarify further on in the paragraph as to why the results of the relationship are not entirely explainable through the selection mechanism activated by the system.

This operation substantiates some links while removing (temporarily) others; it actualizes some possibilities and postpones others.

As already mentioned, meaning provides a key to selection; however, it does not open deterministically identified paths. Instead, "every meaning refers to everything possible, thus to opposing or inconsistent meanings" (Luhmann, 1995, p. 362). As a result, there is a latent potential for inconsistency with the current state, which can include the contradiction in the probability of phenomena, as required by the contemporary epistemology of complexity.

Therefore, theoretically, there is an ample degree of freedom in the choices the enterprise-system can make (accordingly, the possible results of the relationship with the environmental context are even broad), and the greater the potential variety, the more the selection mechanism takes on value, which is also understood as the capability to work with such immense potentialities. To this end, in business theory, both the function of reducing complexity and that of adequate exploitation of this complexity must be attributed the selection process.

This virtually infinite degree of freedom could lead to an entropic scheme if the company were not to use organizational formulas, transitioning toward the creation of a structure,[6] which allows choosing a limited number of alternatives with respect to all existing possibilities, according to mechanisms that are specific to the system in question and that are guided by their meaning: "Structure transforms unstructured complexity into structured complexity" (Luhmann, 1995, p. 282).

Although the reference to distant and inconsistent selections is always possible, the structure limits the relations for the enterprise-system

[6] Maturana and Varela (1980, pp. 19–20; 1987, p. 42) distinguish between organization and structure. The first is the abstract configuration of the relationships that identify a certain class of systems, whereas the second is a description of the components and relationships that constitute a specific system in concrete terms. For example, reference will be made to the organization of a certain number of relationships between parts (legs, backs, and seat) to define a class of chairs to represent something on which it is possible to sit, whereas the structure that is generated by relating certain components (wood and nails rather than plastic and screws) describes a specific chair. "Yet, since a particular organization can be realized by systems with otherwise different structures, the identity of a system may stay invariant while its structure changes within limits determined by its organization. If these limits are overstepped, that is, if the structure of the system changes so that its organization cannot any more be realized, the system loses its identity and the entity becomes something else, a unity defined by another organization" (Maturana & Varela, 1980, p. xx).

through its own mechanism which guarantees autopoiesis. Thus, a scheme is generated that consolidates some selections, making them more likely than others.

In this sense, as has already been mentioned in general for systems, on the one hand, time imposes selection (which would not be necessary if there were an infinite availability of time), and on the other, it acts as a factor of expansion of the possible choices (extension of choice) for the enterprise-system, thereby providing the opportunity to place the selection activities in succession while generating the possibility of deviations at later times. Through the activity of selection, the company creates its identity as a system (or rather, it becomes different due to the specificity of its selective mechanism) and takes risks, in the sense of making a choice among the many possible (and not necessarily the most convenient).

Considering the above, innovative and/or evolutionary selections capable of diverting the reproductive process toward new paths (producing a surprising or unexpected result) may occur. A deviant event generates a disturbance and disappointment of the expectation.[7] If the system reacts by adapting the expectation (thus, the structure) to the situation of disappointment, evolutionary learning is generated, and the enterprise-system deviates toward new reproductive formulas. Conversely, if the system confirms the expectation despite the disappointment, deviation is abandoned and thus learning as well. In the latter case, behavior is always compliant and never deviant, and apparently, greater certainties exist.

The structures that learn can change themselves and their relationship with the outside. This change takes place at the expectations level (and so do the structures as a result). By transforming expectations (structural changes), the company evolves, learns, and reviews its choices, and in the meantime, it reproduces itself. The change can result in a morphogenesis or rather the creation of a new structural form, which can remain consistent with the autopoietic mechanism within certain limits (see previous Note 5).

The representation of structures, as structures of expectations, enables us to examine the interpretation of the results of the micro, meso, and macro relationships in depth and to re-propose a concept that has often

[7] For further information on the concept of expectation, see Luhmann (1995, pp. 292–324).

surfaced during the discussion: the idea that the environment is not an objectifiable reality regardless of the company that relates to it but rather that a part of the context is enacted by the enterprise-system. According to the viewpoint of enactment (Weick, 1979, 1979, 1988; Weick et al., 2005) the company organizes the environment as its reference object and interprets the information that comes from it according to its sensitivity. In this perspective, it is the company that gives meaning to its context. The process of enactment leads to connecting raw data in a certain manner as opposed to another, transforming it into information. Acts permitting such connections are acts of invention rather than discovery and imply a superimposed order rather than an underlying one. As an example of the process of enactment (and the related concept of enacted environment), Weick suggests the experiment wherein musicians from two jazz orchestras try three compositions written by composers who were attributed high or low credibility (Weick et al., 1973). The prediction was that the musicians would find it difficult to assume a logic when a composer was considered as being "non-serious." As a result, they made more mistakes while playing that composer's music, diminished the value of the music, and forgot it faster. However, if the same piece was proposed to an orchestra comparable to the first one but attributing it to a more serious composer, it was expected that musicians would have attributed more value to the music and would have made a greater effort in understanding and remembering it. The expected difference about the errors took place during the first performance of the new music and disappeared during the second. However, the assigned compositions that had been attributed to serious composers were remembered 24 hours after the rehearsal in a much more complete manner. The more focused attention paid to the work of the credible composer resulted in fewer errors and a better performance than the performance of the piece attributed to the non-credible composer. When the musicians believed that the music was of a higher level they generated a better sound musically, due to their increased attention, that conditioned their subsequent performances. The musicians did not react to an environment but activated it.

The enactment is followed by a "selection" and a "retention" phase (see, among others, Weick et al., 2005): the ambiguity that survives after activation is to some extent eliminated through selection, which carries out a sort of retrospective clarification through the conservation of effective representations (to reduce ambiguities) and the elimination of unnecessary representations. Decrease in ambiguity occurs only partially as a selection process that eliminates any ambiguity would imply an impossibility of changing the activated environment, leading to a sterilization of behaviors that would prevent any innovation in external relationships. Lastly, the retention phase enables archiving the activated environments to which the company attributes a usable meaning. What is preserved is a sensible version of the scenario that the ambiguity referred to; however, it would have been possible to create other versions in the presence of the same ambiguities. Thus, the retention process accredits or discredits the environments created in the previous phases.

Retention can affect subsequent activations in the sense that the company remains influenced by the archived activations resulting in a sort of path dependency, which is generated in the relationship that the enterprise-system puts in place with its environmental context.

Worth reiterating, in this case as well, is that the enacted environment, that which presents itself as real, is simply a portion of the possible world, and as the activation depends on the subject that produces the observation, it differs depending on the point of view used.

In the setting we propose, it is assumed that the company as well contributes to generating its environmental context through its representation.[8] The interpretation of the context derives from the enterprise-system's process of description. The latter interprets the environment according to its own cognitive patterns and acts because of this representation. Like all autopoietic systems, the company produces a world or at least gives meaning to a world (Varela, 2007, p. 124).

Thus, the idea that the environment is activated by the company is conceptually opposed to the hypothesis that the latter adapts to an intelligence of the context. With respect to the two extreme positions (that of the predominance of environmental intelligence and the opposite one regarding the supremacy of the enactment mechanism), an interpretation

[8] From the perspective of enactment, we can hypothesize that the company not only interprets the environment by giving it its own representation but also, on the basis of this representation, chooses and acts to make the outlined environment concrete from its point of view (Vicari, 2024, p. 159).

is proposed according to which there is a coevolution between the enterprise-system and its environment via a process of reciprocal adaptation (Rullani & Vicari, 1999, p. 22).

In fact, it has been argued so far that the results of the micro, meso, and macro relationships partially depend on the selective reduction action (compliant or deviant) of the company and the consequential process of activation of the environment set in motion by the company itself. We will now try to clarify why the results of the relationship actually do not depend exclusively on the choices of the enterprise-system. As previously mentioned, companies generate articulated structures to face external complexity and exploit the variety existing in the environmental context, thereby increasing their own complexity. The results of the relationship with the reference environment are somehow linked to the possibility of capturing an increasingly higher degree of external complexity; accordingly, internal complexity increases, and this circumstance entails a shift of the company's attention from the complexity of the environment to its own complexity. Hence, over time, the structure must not only face external complexity but also the growth of the internal complexity. Nevertheless, the establishment of the company as a system also generates an increase in the complexity of the environment as the greater internal organization of the company increases the entropy of the environmental context, according to the principle recalled by von Foerster, for which self-organizing systems "disorganize" their environment (see Sect. 4.1, Chap. 4). The selections of meaning, especially the selections that bring innovation or evolution, not only generate an increase in complexity within the company but also affect the environment. The evolution of the meso- and macroeconomic reference is therefore also generated by the greater complexity of companies that increase their complexity trying to adapt to it. Concurrently, the evolution of the company is generated by the evolution of its meso and macro reference in a process of co-production of the results of the relationship, which operates according to recursive mechanisms like those described with regard to the Boolean networks (see Sect. 1.4.1, Chap. 1). Thus, the company–task environment relationship is reciprocally determined and is perpetrated through a process of "structural coupling" (Maturana & Varela, 1980, pp. 20–21; Maturana & Varela, 1987, p. 75). It presumes interactions of a recurrent and stable nature, whereby each of the two components (the enterprise-system on the one hand and the environment on the other) can trigger changes in the other in a coevolutionary process. The non-existence of a deterministic process leads to a "natural drift" (Maturana & Varela, 1987, pp. 107–117), which defines the results of the company–environment relationship:

> Imagine a hill with a sharp peak. Picture yourself at the top, flicking down drops of water, always in the same direction, even though (because of the mechanics of your action) there are variations in how they begin to fall. Now, imagine that the successive drops are leaving marks on the ground as a record of their fall.
>
> Evidently, if we repeat our experiment many times, we will get slightly different results. Some drops will go straight down; others will meet with obstacles that they will elude in different ways because of their small differences in weight or impetus, going off to one side or the other. The wind may change slightly and move the drops in sinuous ways or away from the initial direction; also, the marks left by previous drops will leave a different surface for subsequent ones, and so on indefinitely.
>
> Let us take this series of experiments and, following the trails left by each drop, let us mark out the paths we have collected … (which) represent the many natural drifts of water drops on the hill, a result of different individual ways of interaction with the irregularities of the land, the wind, and so forth…The hill, of course, is the entire surrounding environment of living beings. It changes through history, partly independent of the way living beings develop and partly dependent on them. (Maturana & Varela, 1987, pp. 107–108)

In other words, even though the enterprise-system contributes to the determination of the results of the micro, meso, and macro relationships through its work of selection and enactment of the environment, it is also subject to the variations determined by other systems present in the environment (e.g., sectoral revolutions due to the movements of other companies). The structural coupling of the autopoietic company, with its own meso- and macroeconomic context, does not presuppose an exchange of provisions but rather mutual solicitations that define the conditions of coevolution and reciprocal adaptation. The interaction generates a result that we can define as a product of the relationship.

To conclude this reasoning, if we take up the underlying argument of this paragraph (the unpredictability of the results of the micro, meso, and macro relationships), the proposed approach suggests giving up a deterministic prediction of the results of the relationship knowing that in all probability, there is more than one possible result. The result that will eventually take place will depend on a number of combined factors: the systemic selection made by the company through its structure, the parallel activation of an environment consistent with its perceptual schemes, the implementation of linked mechanisms in the systems found in the environment (e.g., other companies) that contribute to the evolution of the environmental context, a probable increase in the complexity of both the environment and the company, a reaction to such complexity, and so forth. What remains described is a recursive mechanism whereby, like the Boolean networks illustrated in Sect. 1.4.1, Chap. 1, the configuration of the network at a given time depends on the state of the individual operators and their mutual position even in previous moments in time. As a result, we can frame the unpredictability of the results of the micro, meso, and macro relationships not only in a context of great indeterminacy but also of great openings that are generated by the coevolution of the relationship itself. The results are updated moment-by-moment, and the forecast remains anchored to the vision of the observing company, which has the power to contribute in determining the scenario it envisages to a certain extent.

In this interpretative context, the question should be raised as to what role can be attributed to the most recent tools used to help predict the results of the relationship, such as the research carried out on big data through Artificial Intelligence. Without prejudice to the growing affirmation, with regard to business theory, of reasoning schemes that increasingly consider the probability of the occurrence of different and/or opposing events (flexible budgets, dynamic hyper-segmentation models, procedures based on trial and error mechanisms, correction control systems, and use of options as a criterion for evaluating investment projects), it should be mentioned that the forecasting method contributes to the attribution of meaning by the company to the reference context. The structure that guides the selection process will also constitute its expectations depending on the forecasting method. For example, the company, by analyzing big data, will be guided to a certain extent in activating its surrounding environment and will contribute to the selection and retention processes of some cognitive maps (those that will be considered plausible) while abandoning others. In summary, even the most sophisticated techniques of data analysis support interpretation and must consistently be conceived not as skills that help to unveil an objectively existing reality but rather as ways of supporting the enactment process.

5.5 A Methodological Issue: The Choice of the Observation Point and Construction of Causal Connections

The fourth research topic identified deals with the potential existence of multiple subjective representations of the phenomena studied and the resulting difficulty in defining the parameters that will enable us to judge the reliability and scientific nature of the different points of view. The topic that this paragraph is dedicated to clearly embraces a more universal epistemological question relating to the conditions of objectivity/subjectivity of scientific studies and to a possible coexistence of different hypotheses in the interpretation of a same phenomenon.

It was believed, in the paradigm of classical science, that phenomena could be described based on the absolute criteria of objectivity, whereas in the epistemology of complexity, it is accepted that the representation of reality is also a function of both cognitive maps and the viewing angle of the observing subject. The features of an observed object (in our case, the company or the task environment) depend on the object itself only to a certain extent; they also derive from the position of the observing subject and from the relationship that exists between the observing subject and the object of observation, to the point of making it suitable to consider a larger suprasystem composed of the observed system and the observing system or the system under control and the controller (Beer, 1995, p. 25). To bring the observer closer to the observed object's point of view and limit the subjectivity of the analysis, some scholars, even in a business context (Vicari, 2024, pp. 12–13), encourage a perspective that is similar to that of the system being studied. Despite attributing interest, in the theory of complex social systems, to the observation process from outside the system and recognizing a specific role to scientific analysis[9] in this category, self-observation is identified as a privileged moment of knowledge by the system, emphasizing that it is necessary to match the observation scheme with that in use within the system itself. Although this approach in theory can be shared (it would actually be preferable to capture the systemic point of view as a unitary perspective of observation), the proposed solution appears hardly attainable operationally. The reason being that the observation of the relationship between the company and the environmental context comes from individuals or groups of individuals, who are bearers of their own interpretative maps. These subjects would find it difficult to fully take on the examined system's point of view as none of the observers could give up their individuality in the process of exploration even if they wanted to; moreover, they could not fully share the complexity of the observed systems. The meta systemic point of view, which is ontologically inclusive of some form of absoluteness, cannot be controlled by an observer other than the system itself. As has been mentioned, if individuals are external to the system and are linked to it by interpenetration,[10] they are unable to fully adhere to systemic complexity. Similarly, the system is unable to fully share their complexity (no company completely identifies itself with one or more individuals and no human being exhausts his/her complexity in a company). The unshared portion of either one or the other conceptually excludes the coincidence between the systemic observation and the observation of one or more subjects, regardless of how close they are to the observed system. In other words, the use of the company's point of view appears to be operationally infeasible, both because the observer is *more than* the system and because the system is *more than* the observing subject. The assumption of the company's similar point of view is impeded

[9] In this regard, Luhmann writes: "Scientific analysis is a special case of observation from without, with the special task of acquiring knowledge. It could hardly fulfill its task if it restricted itself to purely analytical distinctions and neglected the fact that within the systems it investigates, processes of self-observation are at work, making the difference between system and environment available within these systems themselves" (Luhmann, 1995, pp. 179–180).

[10] See Sect. 4.3.7, Chap. 4.

by the impossibility for the observer to obtain the globality and individuality of an external and redundant system. Although agreeing with the enterprise-system's elaboration hypothesis of a self-description aimed at its own reproduction, we must accept that such self-description cannot be captured by an external observation process. The approach of those who externally prepare for a process of observation of the micro, meso, and macro relationships is conditioned by their perspective of analysis and interpretative baggage. Researchers, consultants, financiers, managers, entrepreneurs, or any other subjects who approach the observation of the enterprise-system and the relationships that it establishes with its reference context inevitably remain conditioned by both their own means of knowledge and values and by the specific relationship that they create at a given moment between themselves and the observed object (a relationship that is also a function of the purpose of their observation). The external observer cannot fully take on the company's point of view without giving up his own identity (redundant, yet simultaneously deficient in cognitive maps, relationships, and information with respect to that of the observed system).

As a result, the external observation product is influenced by the structure of the observing system. Epistemology of complexity (in the representation of scholars such as Maturana, Varela, and Morin) coherently questions the assumption that "the cognition is a *representation* of an independently existing world" (Capra, 1997, p. 263), to then transition toward a conceptualization according to which cognition contributes to generating phenomenical reality. This generation depends on the structure of the observing organism; therefore, organisms that possess similar structures generate similar worlds.[11] Phenomena previously classified as contradictory, deviant, or inexplicable as they do not respond to a law capable of deciphering them take on new meaning with respect to classical science in an epistemological context based on complexity. To this end, the understanding of phenomena and their cataloging within the law or outside it depends on the structuring of the law itself. A law that, in turn, is derived from the capability of deduction of the observing subject as well as from the characteristics of the observed phenomenon.

[11] For example, human beings share linguistic and conceptual structures due to which they collectively generate their world (Capra, 1997, p. 263).

Frequently, we associate order with the ability to make infallible deductions and disorder with the inability to reach understandable conclusions. However, order and disorder reflect some of our abilities and inabilities and not those of nature (von Foerster cited in Ceruti, 2007, p. 7). Seemingly, some properties that were considered as being part of things turn out to be the observer's properties (von Foerster cited in Ceruti, 2007, p. 7) or of the observer's relationship with the observed object. We cannot prove that what appears to us to be an eventuality is not instead due to our ignorance. On the one hand, we need to note that disorder and chance exist in the universe and play an active role in its evolution. On the other, we are not capable of solving the uncertainty deriving from the notions of disorder and chance (Morin, 2007, p. 26). In this manner, phenomena that are considered highly complex can become understandable if the interpretative code is modified.

The various theoretical perspectives of the micro, meso, and macro relationship[12] is, after all, the testimony of a continuous modification of the decoding keys based on the cognitive objectives of the scholars who produced them. We can take up the distinction between the possible world and the real world from this point of view as well. The world of what is real is the portion of the world of what is possible, which is activated by encountering an observed phenomenon and a vision of it by an observer: a different world could occur if the observer or the conditions of observation were to be changed.

Reintegrating the observer in the micro, meso, and macro relationship description and the parallel presence of multiple points of view mark two fundamental steps in the *Economics of Complexity*. Nevertheless, the recognition of a link between the observer and the product of their observation should not necessarily lead us to take on a position of epistemological anarchism,[13] whereby we cannot refer to any scientific and rational methodology for approaching phenomena and reconstructing the causal relationships between them. The point of view's relativity can be combined with the reliability and rigor of the *method* used; the subjectivity of the analysis, despite not knowing prejudicial structural boundaries, is not

[12] See Chap. 3.

[13] See Sect. 2.5.3, Chap. 2.

identified with arbitrary discretion or abstract fantasy but remains linked to the methodologically correct use of the research instruments applied and the consequentiality of the hypotheses formulated. This topic is of crucial importance for those who aim to approach the study of the company, its complexity, and its relationships with meso- and macroeconomic systems, and it requires attention and an in-depth analysis by anyone whose objective is scientific observation on complex phenomena.

It is worth recalling the thought of another important German sociologist, Max Weber, in this regard. Weber addressed the problem of scientific studies by particularly referring to social phenomena. He provides, in my opinion, a shared cognitive path with regard to combining complexity and methodological rigor.

Weber forms part of the debate that developed in the early twentieth century concerning thc fcatures of natural sciences and historical-social sciences. Weber argued that any scientific method is based on a selection activity as "culture is a finite segment of the meaningless infinity of the world process, a segment on which *human beings* confer meaning and significance" (Weber, 1949, p. 81). Weber states that reality is chaotic and that knowledge is possible due to an evaluation process based on a scale of values, which addresses not only the choice of events but also the meaning to be attributed to them:

> All the analysis of infinite reality which the finite human mind can conduct rests on the tacit assumption that only a finite portion of this reality constitutes the object of scientific investigation, and that only it is "important" in the sense of being "worthy of being known." (Weber, 1949, p. 72)

According to Weber, the values that make knowledge possible are also historically, socially, and even individually relative. The theme of the point of view and the possibility of representation (and of knowledge) of reality as a function of the activation of values and the attribution of meanings returns once again in Weber's analysis. The mediation that makes reality knowable is enabled by "culture," which provides the preconditions for defining the objects of knowledge:

> The number and type of causes which have influenced any given event are always infinite and there is nothing in the things themselves to set some of them apart as only meriting attention ... Order is brought into this chaos only on the condition that in every case only a *part* of concrete reality is interesting and *significant* to us, because only it is related to the *cultural values* with which we approach reality. Only certain sides of the infinitely complex concrete phenomenon, namely those to which we attribute a general *cultural significance* – are therefore worthwhile knowing. They alone are objects of causal explanation. (Weber, 1949, p. 78)

Despite dating back to the initial decades of the last century, the Weberian analysis assumptions are thus perfectly compatible with those indicated as the cornerstones of the new epistemology, which is hardly linked to the search for universal laws capable of explaining the generality of the phenomena.[14]

We thus come to the theme of the method that is of particular interest, whereby Weber does not deny the possibility of identifying laws but affirms that such laws can be used for numerous cases and are not universally valid. Similarly, he does not deny the possibility of ascertaining causal connections to which he attributes the meaning of rules. He believes that this means only isolating some of the contributing factors among the infinite number that create historical-social phenomena.

In Weberian thought, the method guarantees that the historical-social sciences are somehow reliable. Even if the selection upstream of the contributing factors determining a certain event is made based on values, this does not mean that the products of the historical-social sciences are subjective, "in the sense that they are *valid* for one person and not for others" (Weber, 1949, p. 84):

---

[14] It is worth clarifying that Weber distinguishes, in this sense, between natural sciences, to which a certain degree of objectivity should be attributed, and historical-social sciences, where identifying general laws of explanation of phenomena becomes difficult. Weber states: "Laws are important and valuable in the exact natural sciences, in the measure that those sciences are *universally valid.* For the knowledge of historical phenomena in their concreteness, the most general laws, because they are most devoid of content are also the least valuable. The more comprehensive the validity,—or scope—of a term, the more it leads us away from the richness of reality since in order to include the common elements of the largest possible number of phenomena, it must necessarily be as abstract as possible and hence *devoid* of content. In the cultural sciences, the knowledge of the universal or general is never valuable in itself" (Weber, 1949, p. 80).

> Only the degree to which they interest different persons varies. In other words, the choice of the object of investigation and the extent or depth to which this investigation attempts to penetrate into the infinite causal web, are determined by the evaluative ideas which dominate the investigator and his age. In the *method* of investigation, the guiding "point of view" is of great importance for the *construction* of the conceptual scheme which will be used in the investigation. In the mode of their *use*, however, the investigator is obviously bound by the norms of our thought just as much here as elsewhere. (Weber, 1949, p. 84)

The possibility of referring to shared methodologies exists, despite the multiplicity of observation perspectives, plurality of values that guide the research, and diversity of languages used. In this sense, a fundamental step is established by Weber in identifying the *ideal type*, obtained by emphasizing some features of factual events to create abstract representations that help organize the understanding of reality. The ideal type is created by accentuating a connotation and exacerbating a factor that is not found in the absolute state and in conditions of isolation. By instrumentally stressing some significant elements, it provides a unitary conceptual reference to the study:

> The ideal typical concept will help to develop our skill in imputation in *research*: it *is* no "hypothesis" but it offers guidance to the construction of hypotheses. It is not a *description* of reality but it aims to give unambiguous means of expression to such a description...An ideal type is formed by the one-sided *accentuation* of one or more points of view and by the synthesis of a great many diffuse, discrete, more or less present and occasionally absent *concrete individual* phenomena, which are arranged according to those one-sidedly emphasized viewpoints into a unified *analytical* construct (*Gedankenbild*). In its conceptual purity, this mental construct (*Gedankenbild*) cannot be found empirically anywhere in reality. It is a *utopia*. Historical research faces the task of determining in each individual case, the extent to which this ideal-construct approximates to or diverges from reality, to what extent for example, the economic structure of a certain city is to be classified as a "city economy." When carefully applied, those concepts are particularly useful in research and exposition. In very much the same way one can work the "idea" of "handicraft" into a utopia

> by arranging certain traits, actually found in an unclear, confused state in the industrial enterprises of the most different epochs and countries, into a consistent ideal-construct by an accentuation of their essential tendencies. This ideal-type is then related to the idea (*Gedankenausdruck*) which one finds expressed there. One can further delineate a society in which all branches of economic and even intellectual activity are governed by maxims which appear to be applications of the same principle which characterizes the ideal-typical "handicraft" system. Furthermore, one can juxtapose alongside the ideal-typical "handicraft" system the antithesis of a correspondingly ideal-typical capitalistic productive system, which has been abstracted out of certain features of modern large scale industry. On the basis of this, one can delineate the utopia of a "capitalistic" culture, i.e., one in which the governing principle is the investment of private capital. (Weber, 1949, pp. 90–91)

Weber looks at the ideal type as a useful tool for defining categories that do not correspond to a concrete reality but which "moves at least one step away from it" (Coser, 2012, p. 223), starting from the impossibility of reconstructing reality in its entirety through any conceptual framework. It allows the researcher to establish a parameter that enables studying affinities and deviations, while providing a method for a comparative study.

As a result, the method can be heuristic in the *Economics of Complexity*. As Beer (1995, pp. 52–53) suggests, the heuristic method is opposed to the algorithm. The algorithm is a set of instructions to achieve an objective, whereas the heuristic method is a set of instructions for the search of an unknown objective through a study that continuously and repeatedly evaluates the progress made according to a certain criterion:

> An algorithm is a technique, or a mechanism, which prescribes how to reach a fully specified goal. A typical air pilot's flight-plan is an algorithm... A method for finding the square root is an algorithm, and so is a computer program...The programmer has to write an algorithm, then, which will exactly determine the computer's next move in any set of circumstances whatever...An heuristic specifies a method of behaving which will tend towards a goal which cannot be precisely specified because we know *what* it is but not *where* it is. Suppose you are trying to reach the peak of a

> conical mountain enveloped in cloud. It must have a higher point, but you do not know the compass bearing. The instruction: "keep going up", will get you there, wherever "there" is…Heuristics prescribe general rules for reaching general goals, then, and do not typically prescribe an exact route to a located goal as does an algorithm…To think in terms of heuristics rather than algorithms is at once a way of coping with proliferating variety. Instead of trying to organize it in full detail, you organize it only somewhat; you then ride on the dynamics of the system in the direction you want to go. (Beer, 1995, pp. 52–53)

The transition from a methodology based on the algorithm to a methodology based on heuristics indicates a fundamental step that has led to refer to the new epistemology using expressions such as "epistemology of complexity" (Morin et al., 1984) or "genetic epistemology" (Piaget, 1970). Normative epistemology aims to construct a unitary body of knowledge, through conditions of validity that disregard time and space while epistemology of complexity promotes studies aimed at understanding how the norm is generated through consistently mobile information that is linked to the development of phenomena.

It would be inconsistent to delve further into the topic of scientific observation methods in the *Economics of Complexity* through this work because it would mean focusing on an issue that needs enrichment and instruments greater than those put forth so far. In this scenario, the order is not pre-existing but is derived from a process of methodological systematization. Knowledge is based on value choices in terms of languages, selected contributing causes, and the chosen observation perspective in general and is produced by building, downstream, a coherent sequence of causal relationships that—highlighting some instrumentally unilateral characteristics of the phenomena (ideal type)—guide the creation of scenarios that could be defined as scientifically correct. Here, reference is made to a coherence within the process that is initiated and is addressed by the choices made upstream rather than a universal method that can be applied in any circumstance.

The definition of the objects of study, the identification of their mutual boundaries, and the study of the results of the relationship itself are not issues that can be solved in an absolute sense and once and for all in the micro, meso, and macro relationships. It depends both on what we identify as an observed system at a given time and the link that the latter establishes with a reference context. This implies that once a choice has been made concerning the usable perspective (e.g., to look at the relationship by identifying a certain network of firms as a unit of inquiry), it becomes necessary not only to maintain a vision that is coherent with that choice but, above all, to clearly state the cognitive objectives. Coherency does not manifest itself by adopting a universal model of representation of reality; rather, it takes concrete form through the perspective of observation, through the transparency of the hypotheses' values underlying the methodological path, and through the logical construction of causal sequences.

This vision implicates a radical change of the idea that there can be a progressive increase in knowledge until complete, unitary, and objective knowledge of the phenomena under observation is reached. An approach to a fully reconstructible scientific scenario does not exist. Instead, as new analysis perspectives are created, new cognitive possibilities are unlocked and further paths of research develop. There is no gradual approach to conditions of increasingly complete knowledge but an enhancement of possible perspectives based on multiple hypotheses and visions. A moment of definitive knowledge does not exist, just as there is no custodian point of view of a global synthesis. Instead, there is a ceaseless production of perspectives that reciprocally enrich and refer to each other and that somehow can be connected.

The various interpretations of the micro, meso, and macro relationships that have been given historically are neither unifiable in a single meta-proposal nor the interpretation contained in this work aim to be. Instead, it becomes important to historicize the visions, focus on the contaminations, and identify the movements that either internally or externally have produced an opening toward complexity (marked as "turning points" in Chap. 3). The various theoretical perspectives used in economic studies to describe the company–task environment relationship push for a different interpretation of phenomena according to the conceptual approach that inspires them and the observation conditions in which the scholars who proposed them find themselves; however, they simultaneously refer to and complement each other.

References

Beer, S. (1995). *Brain of the Firm. The Managerial Cybernetics of Organization* (2nd ed.). John Wiley & Sons.

Capra, F. (1997). *The Web of Life. A New Synthesis of Mind and Matter.* HarperCollins Publishers.

Ceruti, M. (2007). La hybris dell'omniscienza e la sfida della complessità. In G. Bocchi & M. Ceruti (Eds.), *La sfida della complessità.* Bruno Mondadori Editori.

Coser, L. A. (2012). *Masters of Sociological Thought. Ideas in Historical and Social Context.* Rawat Publications.

Luhmann, N. (1995). *Social Systems.* Standford University Press.

Maturana, H. R., & Varela, F. J. (1980). *Autopoiesis and Cognition. The Realization of Living.* D. Reidel Publishing Company.

Maturana, H. R., & Varela, F. J. (1987). *The Tree of Knowledge. The Biological Roots of Human Understanding.* Shambhala Publications.

Morin, E. (2007). Le vie della complessità. In G. Bocchi & M. Ceruti (Eds.), *La sfida della complessità.* Bruno Mondadori Editori.

Morin, E., Atias, C., & Le Moigne, J. L. (1984). *Science et Conscience de la Complexité. Echanges avec Edgar Morin.* Libraire de l'Université.

Piaget, J. (1970). *L'epistémologie génétique.* Presses universitaires de France.

Rullani, E., & Vicari, S. (1999). Introduzione. In E. Rullani & S. Vicari (Eds.), *Sistemi ed evoluzioni nel management.* Etas.

Varela, J. V. (2007). Complessità del cervello e autonomia del vivente. In G. Bocchi & M. Ceruti (Eds.), *La sfida della complessità.* Bruno Mondadori Editori.

Vicari, S. (2024). *The Living Firm. Journey into a Different Conception.* Amazon Publishing.

von Foerster, H. (2003). On Self-Organizing Systems and their Environments. In H. von Foerster (Ed.), *Understanding Understanding. Essays on Cybernetics and Cognition.* Springer Verlag.

von Foerster, H. (2007). Cibernetica ed epistemologia: storia e prospettive. In G. Bocchi & M. Ceruti (Eds.), *La sfida della complessità.* Bruno Mondadori Editori.

Weber, M. (1949). "Objectivity" in Social Science and Social Policy. In E. A. Shils & H. A. Finch (Eds.), *Max Weber on The Methodology of the Social Sciences.* The Free Press of Glencoe.

Weick, K. E. (1979a). Enactment Processes in Organizations. In M. S. Barry & G. R. Salancik (Eds.), *New Directions in Organizational Behaviour*. St. Clair Press.

Weick, K. E. (1979b). *The Social Psychology of Organizing* (2nd ed.). McGraw-Hill.

Weick, K. E. (1988). Enacted Sense Making in Crisis Situation. *Journal of Management Studies, 25*(4), 305–317.

Weick, K. E., Gilfillan, D. P., & Keith, T. A. (1973). The Effect of Composer Credibility on Orchestra Performance. *Sociometry, 36*(4), 435–462.

Weick, K. E., Sutcliffe, K. M., & Obstfeld, D. (2005). Organizing and the Process of Sensemaking. *Organization Science, 16*(4), 409–421.

6

Conclusions

Abstract From the Management's point of view, one of the most interesting results of the vision based on the "complex systems' theoretical perspective" is the impact it has on the governance of the company. In this perspective, we have, on the one hand, the discretionary scope, which increases excessively, in so much as nothing is prejudicially prevented and the "references of meaning" consistently open probabilities, even to deviant or contradictory choices; on the other hand, the results of the micro, meso, and macro relationship are not determined exclusively by whoever is responsible for governing the company; they are also determined by systemic and intersystemic mechanisms which—incessantly selecting certain possibilities and not others—generate paths that go beyond the control of individuals. To a certain extent, the company adapts to the complexity of the environment; in contrast, as it becomes increasingly more complex, it focuses on its own complexity and contributes to making the context more complex in a co-evolutionary relationship that radically changes the conceptualization of the decision-making function. In this conceptual context, the decision-making processes must be capable of tolerating the uncertainty linked to the complexity and unknowability of the systemic reality in its entirety.

C. Mazzoni, *Firms, Industries, Markets*, https://doi.org/10.1007/978-3-031-59823-4_6

Keywords Decision-making and governance of the company in the *Economics of Complexity* • Interpenetration between the individual and the company as a key to understanding decision-making processes • The renunciation of subjective hegemony over systemic and intersystemic relationships in the *Economics of Complexity*

6.1 Decision-Making and Governance of the Company in the *Economics of Complexity*

From the management's point of view, one of the most interesting results of the vision based on the complex systems' theoretical perspective is the impact it has on the governance of the company. In this perspective, we have, on the one hand, the discretionary scope, which increases excessively, in so much as nothing is prejudicially prevented and the references of meaning, as we have seen, consistently open probabilities, even to deviant or contradictory choices; on the other hand, the results of the micro, meso, and macro relationship are not determined exclusively by whoever is responsible for governing the company; they are also determined by systemic and intersystemic mechanisms which—incessantly selecting certain possibilities and not others—generate paths that go beyond the control of individuals. Complexity becomes defined with respect to the objects of study, and the decision-making processes can only be generated within this premise. To a certain extent, the company adapts to the complexity of the environment; in contrast, as it becomes increasingly more complex, it focuses on its own complexity and contributes to making the context more complex in a co-evolutionary relationship that radically changes the conceptualization of the decision-making function. Moreover, from this perspective, it is necessary to raise awareness among decision-makers regarding the self-observation process of the company, which is created as part of the micro, meso, and macro relationship, and, consequently, on the dual role it plays as an observed and observing system. In this conceptual context, the decision-making processes must be capable of tolerating the uncertainty linked to the complexity and unknowability of the systemic reality in its entirety.

In other words, the potential field of action in the complex systems' theoretical perspective is highest although control over the results of the relationship is reduced.

On the one hand, the ability of the top strategic management to have an impact appears to decrease because of the limited predictability of the company-task environment co-evolution; on the other hand, the system's possibility of action is infinitely expanded in navigating toward every possible option. In such a perspective, the decision is the selection of a state among all those possible (Beer, 1995, p. 212) and not the choice of an optimal state. Consequently, the effect of the governance process leads to the incessant opening of potential scenarios rather than the definition of perfectly predefined routes. The uncertainty regarding the results of the choices constitutes an essential corollary of the complexity of the micro, meso, and macro relationship. In a representation of the relationship, such as the one being proposed, uncertainty is indeed a structural condition intrinsically linked to the vision of the gap of complexity that exists between the enterprise-system and its environment. If uncertainty were to be eliminated, the structures[1] would no longer have any reason to exist as they have the task of guaranteeing the reproduction of the system in situations of unpredictability (Luhmann, 1995, p. 288).

6.2 Interpenetration Between the Individual and the Company as a Key to Understanding Decision-Making Processes

In this scenario, it is worth returning to and examining the connection between the enterprise-system and the decision-makers. To better understand the micro, meso, and macro relationship in systemic rationality, it is, therefore, necessary to return, albeit briefly, to the conceptualization of the individual–company relationship. According to Rullani and Vicari (1999, p. 11), most economists, including business economists, consider

---

[1] Regarding the role of the structure in the complex systems' theoretical perspective, see Sect. 5.4, Chap. 5.

people to be part of the enterprise-system. However, the authors state that it is necessary to assume that the company is not made up of individuals, who are a different logical category from organizations; in fact, the individual is an immense universe that cannot be reduced to being a component of a company. If the individuals are considered an external entity concerning the company, as suggested by Rullani and Vicari, they do not constitute one of the elements of the enterprise-system. Instead, they represent an autonomous system with a completely peculiar relationship with the company (the interpenetration), which presupposes the distinct autopoiesis of both even when under conditions of a strong link (see Sect. 4.3.7, Chap. 4). We believe, in this regard, that the appropriation of the concept of interpenetration by business theory can offer a clear explanation of the relationship generated between human beings and firms in the complex systems' theoretical perspective. As has already been mentioned, while in the humanistic tradition, social systems could be interpreted as aggregations of individuals, in the Luhmannian conception, the distinction of human beings in relation to the systems in which they participate prompts the representation of the individual as a distinct system with respect to the enterprise-system. Likewise, social systems (and therefore also enterprises) cannot be reduced to individual consciousness, nor can they be interpreted as resulting from a summation between the consciences of several individuals (Luhmann, 1995, p. 438). The individual, however, *penetrates* the social system, introducing his/her complexity (or rather, a portion of his/her complexity) for the construction of the enterprise. In turn, the latter *penetrates* the individual by making available to the individual-system a part of its systemic complexity. In the interpenetration relationship, the behaviors of the systems are co-determined. This occurs because the infinite complexity of the two systems (individual and enterprise) makes it impossible to share their mutual totality. There is no belonging of the individual to the company in this conceptualization: the two systems remain autonomous and independent, respond to distinct autopoietic logics, and adhere to the relationship of mutual penetration.

However, it is necessary to recall a fundamental step to share the understanding of this representation. As previously mentioned, the interpenetration relationship is not only a generic connection but also a *constitutive* relationship for the systems that participate in it. The relationship that arises because of the interpenetration between individuals and enterprise does not presuppose—as has been said—a simple exchange of information and systemic spaces; it implies the reciprocal availability of the systems in question (individuals and enterprise) to participate in the formation of each other, making available a fraction of their complexity while using a part of the complexity of the other system. The representation of the individual as being external to the system does not, therefore, mean the exclusion or alienation of the individual from the enterprise-system. Rather, it is a necessary logical step, albeit difficult to accept, to represent the noncoincidence of the enterprise with the consciousness of an individual or a group of individuals (the group, in turn, does not have a single conscience but decides based on complex mechanisms of interrelation[2]) and the parallel impossibility of the individual as being completely part of a system, which, with all evidence, constitutes only a fraction (more or less large) of his/her complexity.

As a result, we reiterate that the proposed representation does not diminish the importance of the individual in the life of the company but recognizes that the individual is a different system, which participates, in addition to the company, simultaneously with multiple social systems (defined precisely to distinguish them from biological ones), of a family, political, religious, or playful nature. Reducing the individual to a mere component of the enterprise is a denial of his/her complexity, and, at the same time, a non-admission of the enterprise's systemic complexity.

6.3 The Renunciation of Subjective Hegemony Over Systemic and Intersystemic Relationships in the *Economics of Complexity*

Stemming from the proposed conceptualization is a vision of the position of the individuals responsible for the governance of the company, which differs, in certain respects, from what is more consolidated in business theory.

[2] On the issue of conflict or agreement between individuals in decision-making processes see, among others, the concepts of "coalitions of groups" by Cyert and March (1963) and "organized anarchies" by Cohen et al. (1972).

The representation of companies as systems that, in an attempt to tackle the complexity of the environment, increase their complexity is scarcely compatible with the idea that an individual (or a group) can guide the overall organization and its relationships, unequivocally directing its path. According to Vicari (2024, p. 41), this circumstance is demonstrated by the fact that even in companies with a well-identified ownership and a strict hierarchical order, no leader can truly control the organization; rather, they can only try to influence it. The hypothesis of a hetero-directed development of the system does not harmonize with the co-evolutionary vision: the top management, which faces the dual difficulty of having to manage the difference in complexity stemming from the comparison with the outside and the unpredictability of the connections activated by the internal structures to cope with this difference, is unable to perfectly control the results of the micro, meso, and macro relationship.

In fact, in a representation whereby the company and the human beings do not reciprocally use their entire complexity, no individual (or group of individuals) can fully capture the systemic nature of the organization, nor can they completely govern, through their choices, the direction that the system will take in its relationship with the outside.[3] It is difficult, if the proposed representation is accepted, to imagine that there is a perfect cause–effect relationship between government action and the result produced as the initial impulse reflects a series of interdependencies, in its systemic path, that make the outcome difficult to predict.

Nevertheless, it is not our aim to deny the existence of a governing body in companies or to ignore the importance of the role played by these bodies. Rather, we wish to discuss a revision of the concept of governance imagined by business studies to arrive at the acceptance of a

[3] Moreover, "interpenetration is a state of affairs that varies historically" (Luhmann, 1995, p. 252), whereby the relationship established between the enterprise-system and the individuals is modified depending on the development of the mutual relationship. It follows that, over time, the mutual influences change based on the generation of intersystemic links between the company and the human beings that participate in it. Additionally, the enterprise-individual link is transformed thanks to variations that occur in the connections between the various individuals who participate in the life of the company.

management model that is more in line with the complexity of the micro, meso, and macro relationship and with systemic and intersystemic rationality.[4]

On the importance of the top management, it should be made clear that within the interpretation relationship, a different capacity of influence of individuals on the system and the micro, meso, and macro relationship arises, depending on the position they hold within the company. In other words, there is a different force of interpenetration depending on the position of the individual in the company's organization. If it is true that both an employee and a CEO are connected to the company via the interpretation relationship, the second subject's influence on the business–task environment relationship is greater than that of the first. This also takes place because individuals with greater access to power likely have more success in enacting their vision of the organization, such as individuals heard by those in power (consultants, committees, and project teams, among others) that generate a process of "binding" and "persuasive" enactment (Weick, 1979, p. 168).[5]

Regarding the opportunity of producing instruments to operate in the context described, it is perhaps appropriate to include complexity in the interpretative baggage with which to equip both managers and entrepreneurs when they are trained. Should the representation of the company as a complex system be shared, the leaders will have to develop a governance mentality that moves away from the anthropocentric vision of the organization and the possibility of total direction and control of the micro, meso, and macro relationship. Instead, they will need to develop sensitivity toward systemic and intersystemic logics, renouncing the mirage of omniscient management. It is a question of detaching oneself

[4] The systemic rationality is not the result of the choices of some individuals; rather, it is the result of the relationships established between all the components of the system (Vicari, 2024, p. 47). In this sense, corporate behavior is neither the sum nor the average of individual decisions, nor the outcome of a collective process of making choices. "Instead, the behavior of a business emerges from a myriad of factors: ongoing interactions, signal exchanges, individual computations, personal biases and expectations, shared norms, procedural protocols, organizational mechanism, and more" (Vicari, 2024, p. 60).

[5] It is worth clarifying that the imposition by an individual, or a group of individuals, of activation, is linked by Weick to a position of substantial power rather than to the simple hierarchical placement within the organization.

from the hypothesis of governing bodies (whether individual or collective) with the possibility of complete domination, an increasingly less defensible hypothesis in phenomenical reality, aimed at approaching an acentric vision typical of contemporary science (Luhmann, 1995, p. 439), and of acceptance of mutual interdependencies. The ability to learn from experimentation, the capacity to tolerate error and contradiction, and the acceptance of imperfection and unpredictability are some of the lessons that managers, entrepreneurs, and even university students should be taught. From this perspective, training programs are often inadequate, even those that appear to be the most advanced worldwide.[6] Individuals who work or aspire to work in companies must reflect on the diversity of their experiences and be encouraged by the pluralism of their potential choices.[7]

As a result, the change in perspective of the micro, meso, and macro relationship, according to the logic of systemic complexity, requires a conceptual review of the power of influence of individuals in determining events. No company (nor any individual or group of individuals) "possesses enough complexity to react 'systematically' to everything that occurs" (Luhmann, 1995, p. 183).

The logic of governance in the paradigm of systemic rationality renounces subjective hegemony over systemic and intersystemic relations. This hegemony, on paper, has given individuals immense power, whereas, in everyday life, it has imposed on them a particular sense of frustration in facing the complexity and unpredictability of business life. We need a new way of thinking regarding the future that recognizes reality as a construction that is never definitive, that treats uncertainty not as the worst enemy but as the best ally, and that considers the proliferation of ideas, approaches, and actions not as an unnecessary dispersion of energy but as the only viable way to build new possibilities (Bocchi & Ceruti, 2007, p. XXXVI).

[6] On the subject, see Mintzberg and Gosling (2002).

[7] "The hardest lesson for business school professors to learn, ourselves included, is that experienced managers have at least as much to learn from each other as they do from us" (Mintzberg & Gosling, 2002, p. 67).

References

Beer, S. (1995). *Brain of the Firm. The Managerial Cybernetics of Organization* (2nd ed.). John Wiley & Sons.

Bocchi, G., & Ceruti, M. (2007). Introduzione. La sfida della complessità nell'era globale. In G. Bocchi & M. Ceruti (Eds.), *La sfida della complessità.* Bruno Mondadori Editori.

Cohen, M. D., March, J. G., & Olsen, J. P. (1972). A Garbage Can Model of Organizational Chioce. *Administrative Science Quarterly, 17*(1), 1–25.

Cyert, R. M., & March, J. G. (1963). *A Behavioural Theory of the Firm.* Prentice Hall.

Luhmann, N. (1995). *Social Systems.* Standford University Press.

Mintzberg, H., & Gosling, J. (2002). Educating Managers Beyond Borders. *Academy of Management Learning & Education, 1*(1), 64–76.

Rullani, E., & Vicari, S. (1999). Introduzione. In E. Rullani & S. Vicari (Eds.), (1999) *Sistemi ed evoluzioni nel management.* Etas.

Vicari, S. (2024). *The Living Firm. Journey into a Different Conception.* Amazon Publishing.

Weick, K. E. (1979). *The Social Psychology of Organizing* (2nd ed.). McGraw-Hill.

Index[1]

[1] Note: Page numbers followed by 'n' refer to notes.

C. Mazzoni, *Firms, Industries, Markets*, https://doi.org/10.1007/978-3-031-59823-4

SPRINGER NATURE

GPSR Compliance

The European Union's (EU) General Product Safety Regulation (GPSR) is a set of rules that requires consumer products to be safe and our obligations to ensure this.

If you have any concerns about our products, you can contact us on ProductSafety@springernature.com

In case Publisher is established outside the EU, the EU authorized representative is:

Springer Nature Customer Service Center GmbH
Europaplatz 3
69115 Heidelberg, Germany

The manufacturer's authorised representative in the EU is Springer Nature Customer Service Centre GmbH, Europaplatz 3, 69115 Heidelberg, Germany. If you have any concerns regarding our products, please contact ProductSafety@springernature.com

Printed and bound by CPI Group (UK) Ltd, Croydon, CR0 4YY
01/10/2026
02225879-0013